Wired Differently, Loving Stronger

A Relationship Guide for the Neurospicy and Their Partners,

for Better Understanding, Support, and Love

Nicci Brochard
&
Dr. Ben Chuba

Wired Differently, Loving Stronger

A Relationship Guide for the Neurospicy and Their Partners,

for Better Understanding, Support, and Love

CROSSBORDER

New York, London, Quebec

Contents

Introduction

Relationships often come with their own complexities, there are unique dynamics that arise when neurodivergence intersects with love and partnership. For those who identify as "neurospicy" — a term lovingly adopted to describe individuals with neurodivergent traits, such as ADHD, autism, dyslexia, and other neurological conditions — the way they experience the world can differ drastically from those who are neurotypical. And while this diversity in brain wiring may pose some challenges, it also brings depth, creativity, and profound love to the table.

"Wired Differently, Loving Stronger: A Relationship Guide for the Neurospicy and Their Partners, for Better Understanding, Support, and Love" is an essential resource designed to help both neurodivergent individuals and their partners navigate the intricacies of love in a neurodiverse relationship. It is not merely a how-to manual for solving problems, but a compassionate and insightful journey into the hearts and minds of those who are wired differently. This guide offers a comprehensive exploration of how neurodivergence shapes relationships, how it can lead to powerful bonds, and how to create a stronger, more understanding partnership through mutual respect, communication, and unwavering support.

For those in relationships where one or both partners are neurodivergent, the experience can be one of both beautiful triumphs and painful misunderstandings. The key to overcoming these challenges lies in fostering empathy and a willingness to learn, adapt, and grow together. The aim of this book is to provide an informative, yet emotionally enriching approach to understanding and supporting each other in neurodiverse relationships.

The book opens with an exploration of what it truly means to be "neurospicy." It goes beyond the surface-level definitions of ADHD, autism, and other neurodivergent conditions, and instead delves into the lived experiences of individuals who embody these traits. You will gain insights into the sensory overloads, the often misunderstood social cues, the moments of brilliance, and the occasional frustrations that come with neurodivergence. By gaining a deeper understanding of these experiences, both neurodivergent individuals and their partners can work towards a more empathetic connection.

One of the fundamental concepts explored in this guide is the importance of communication. Neurodivergent individuals may express themselves, process emotions, or interpret the world around them differently. This can lead to potential conflicts in relationships when one partner struggles to comprehend the other's perspective. "Wired Differently, Loving Stronger" offers practical tools and strategies for both partners to improve communication, develop patience, and create a safe space for honest and open dialogue.

Support is another central theme of this book. Neurodivergent individuals often require different types of support from their partners, whether it be in managing daily tasks, coping with emotional regulation, or providing a stable and understanding environment. Partners, in turn, need tools to support their loved ones without losing sight of their own needs and well-being. By learning to strike a balance between being supportive and maintaining personal boundaries, couples can create an environment where both individuals feel heard, valued, and loved.

Love in a neurodiverse relationship is not a one-size-fits-all model. It is nuanced and multi-faceted, with its own rhythms and expressions. As you read through this guide, you will uncover the ways in which neurodivergence enriches love by encouraging creativity, authenticity, and emotional depth. Rather than viewing differences as obstacles, the book encourages partners to celebrate these differences as strengths — qualities that make the relationship uniquely theirs.

In the end, "Wired Differently, Loving Stronger" is not just a relationship guide; it is a celebration of love in all its forms, challenges, and triumphs. It is a call to embrace the beauty of neurodivergence, to learn from each other, and to build a partnership that transcends the ordinary, where both individuals are supported, loved, and allowed to thrive in their unique ways. Whether you're navigating the complexities of a neurodiverse relationship or simply seeking to deepen your understanding of your partner's world, this book offers a roadmap to a love that is stronger, more resilient, and far more beautiful than ever imagined.

Nicci and I (Ben) thank you immensely for choosing our book. We promise you will find in it what you are looking for.

Chapter 1

Love in the Neurospicy Lane

Why Loving Differently Isn't Wrong—It's Revolutionary

In relationships, there is no universal manual. Every couple, regardless of their backgrounds, experiences, and individual traits, must navigate the ebb and flow of love in their own unique way. However, when neurodivergence enters the equation, the dynamics of love can feel like an entirely new world—a world where the rules are unwritten, and the path forward is unclear. Neurodivergent individuals—those whose brains are wired differently due to conditions like ADHD, autism, dyslexia, and more—often find themselves misunderstood in relationships. In many ways, these individuals are taught that their differences are something to be corrected, a deviation from the norm that needs to be 'fixed.'

But what if loving differently isn't wrong? What if it's revolutionary?

This chapter will explore what it means to love in the neurospicy lane—a term that reclaims the idea of neurodivergence and embraces it with warmth, creativity, and empowerment. Neurodivergence is not a deficit or a flaw but an opportunity for growth, a gateway to innovation, and, most importantly, a path to a love that's stronger, deeper, and more authentic. It's not just about managing challenges; it's about embracing the gifts that neurodivergent individuals bring to relationships. By setting the tone with radical empathy, communication, and curiosity, we can move away from the misunderstandings and myths surrounding neurodivergent love and move toward a partnership built on understanding and mutual respect.

Defining Neurodivergence in the Context of Relationships

Neurodivergence is a term that has gained increasing visibility in recent years. Simply put, it refers to the idea that some individuals' brains work differently from what is typically considered "standard" or "neurotypical." Neurodivergence can encompass a wide range of conditions, including Attention Deficit Hyperactivity Disorder (ADHD), Autism Spectrum Disorder (ASD), dyslexia, dyscalculia, and other cognitive variations.

In the context of relationships, neurodivergence refers to how individuals who are neurodivergent navigate emotional and interpersonal dynamics differently. While everyone experiences relationships uniquely, neurodivergent individuals might approach communication, emotional regulation, social cues, and intimacy in ways that differ from the societal norm. But this isn't a flaw—it's an alternative way of seeing and experiencing the world, which can offer profound insights and creative solutions.

For example, a partner with ADHD may have trouble staying focused on conversations or completing household tasks in a timely manner. This may be misunderstood as carelessness or irresponsibility. However, with an understanding of ADHD, a partner might see this behavior not as an intentional fault but as a challenge to be managed with empathy, communication, and structure. Similarly, a partner on the autism spectrum might have a tendency to prefer solitary activities or struggle with eye contact, but these behaviors don't reflect a lack of love; rather, they are different expressions of connection.

In relationships, recognizing and respecting these differences is crucial for creating an environment of understanding and support. Neurodivergence isn't something to be fixed; it's a different way of loving. When partners understand this, they can build a foundation that allows both individuals to thrive in their own unique ways.

What "Neurospicy" Really Means (A Warm, Empowering Take)

The term "neurospicy" is a playful, endearing way to describe neurodivergent individuals. It's a celebration of being a little different, a little outside the box, and not conforming to the norms set by society. "Spicy" implies that there's an exciting, dynamic element to the person, that they add something extra to the relationship—something that's bold, vibrant, and full of flavor.

Neurospicy doesn't just mean being quirky or unpredictable, though these traits may certainly be present. It's an empowering term that captures the essence of embracing one's neurodivergence with pride. The term encourages self-acceptance and celebrates individuality. Rather than viewing neurodivergence as something that must be hidden or erased, "neurospicy" is about owning it, enjoying it, and using it as a tool for growth and connection.

For those in relationships with neurospicy individuals, this term serves as a reminder to approach these partners with curiosity and respect, rather than judgment. It highlights the unique perspectives and attributes that neurodivergent individuals bring to relationships—perspectives that often lead to innovation, creative problem-solving, and a deeper emotional connection. The beauty of being neurospicy is that it's not about fitting into a predefined mold. It's about creating your own space and setting your own rules, all while building a love that is supportive, authentic, and profoundly rewarding.

The Unique Strengths and Gifts of Neurodivergent Partners

While neurodivergence may come with challenges, it also brings unique strengths and gifts that can enhance any relationship. In fact, many neurodivergent individuals possess exceptional skills that can be deeply beneficial in a partnership.

1. **Creativity and Innovation**: Many neurodivergent individuals are exceptionally creative, offering fresh perspectives and innovative solutions to problems. Whether it's coming up with a unique approach to a household task, solving a conflict in an unexpected way, or creating something entirely new, neurodivergent partners often bring fresh, out-of-the-box thinking to the relationship.

2. **Hyperfocus**: Individuals with ADHD, for instance, may experience periods of hyperfocus, during which they can immerse themselves deeply in a task or project. While this can

sometimes lead to distractions in other areas, it can also result in exceptional productivity and accomplishment, especially when it comes to projects that require intense concentration.

3. **Authenticity and Honesty**: Many neurodivergent individuals tend to be straightforward and honest, often valuing transparency in relationships. This can foster a sense of trust and openness that is critical for building a strong partnership.

4. **Empathy and Sensitivity**: Contrary to some misconceptions, many neurodivergent individuals possess a deep sense of empathy. In fact, some individuals on the autism spectrum or with ADHD are highly sensitive to the emotions of others and are deeply affected by the feelings of those around them. This emotional awareness can lead to profound connections in relationships, as these individuals often go above and beyond to understand and care for their partners.

5. **Resilience**: Neurodivergent individuals often develop a high level of resilience. Having faced and overcome the challenges of navigating a world that is not designed for them, they bring a strength of character to their relationships. They have learned to adapt, problem-solve, and persevere, skills that are invaluable when navigating the complexities of love.

While these strengths can create a rich and fulfilling partnership, they also require understanding and support from both partners. Neurodivergent individuals may not always have the same coping mechanisms or ways of expressing their emotions as their neurotypical counterparts. By embracing their unique strengths, however, both partners can create a relationship that celebrates these qualities and fosters growth.

Common Relationship Misunderstandings and Myths

When neurodivergent individuals enter relationships, they often face a series of misunderstandings and myths that can create tension or confusion. These misconceptions are usually rooted in a lack of awareness or an incomplete understanding of neurodivergence. Let's take a look at some of the most common myths and how they can be addressed:

1. **Myth: Neurodivergent individuals don't understand emotions.** While it's true that some neurodivergent individuals may struggle with recognizing or expressing emotions in the traditional way, this doesn't mean they lack empathy or emotional depth. In fact, many neurodivergent individuals have a profound emotional capacity but express it in different ways. It's crucial for both partners to communicate openly about how they experience emotions and to find ways to express care that work for both individuals.

2. **Myth: Neurodivergent people don't want intimacy.** Another common misconception is that neurodivergent individuals don't crave emotional or physical intimacy. This myth often stems from the assumption that neurodivergent individuals are inherently cold or distant, particularly those on the autism spectrum. In reality, many neurodivergent individuals long for deep emotional

connections, but they may express this longing in ways that are less conventional. Partners need to recognize these expressions of intimacy and respond with love and curiosity.

3. **Myth: Neurodivergence is a problem that needs to be fixed.** This myth is perhaps the most harmful. It positions neurodivergence as something inherently wrong or broken. The truth is, neurodivergence is simply a different way of being. It is not something that requires fixing but rather something that requires understanding and adaptation. In relationships, both partners should focus on accepting one another for who they are, rather than trying to change each other.

Setting the Tone: Radical Empathy, Communication, and Curiosity

The foundation of any successful relationship is built on empathy, communication, and curiosity. This is especially true in neurodivergent partnerships, where understanding one another's experiences and needs is key.

- **Radical Empathy**: Radical empathy goes beyond surface-level understanding. It requires fully embracing and respecting the other person's experiences, even if they are vastly different from your own. In neurodivergent relationships, radical empathy involves acknowledging that each partner's brain works differently and that these differences are not flaws, but opportunities for growth.

- **Communication**: Clear and open communication is vital. Neurodivergent individuals may have unique ways of processing information or expressing themselves. For instance, someone with ADHD may struggle with short-term memory, while someone on the autism spectrum may not recognize certain social cues. Both partners should make an effort to communicate in ways that are clear, concise, and respectful, always checking in with each other to ensure mutual understanding.

- **Curiosity**: Curiosity is a powerful tool in neurodivergent relationships. Instead of jumping to conclusions or making assumptions, both partners should cultivate a genuine curiosity about each other's experiences. This means asking questions, learning about each other's neurodivergent traits, and being open to new ways of thinking and feeling. Curiosity allows both partners to grow together, fostering a relationship that is ever-evolving and resilient.

Conclusion

Loving in the neurospicy lane isn't just about managing challenges or overcoming obstacles—it's about embracing a new way of being in love. Neurodivergent relationships offer a rich tapestry of unique strengths, gifts, and opportunities for growth. When both partners approach the relationship with radical empathy, open communication, and a genuine curiosity about one another's experiences, love can flourish in ways that are not only fulfilling but revolutionary.

By understanding and celebrating neurodivergence, partners can build relationships that are authentic, compassionate, and incredibly rewarding. The journey may be different from the one that society often expects, but it is one that can lead to a deeper, more meaningful connection. As you move through this guide, you'll discover how to embrace and nurture the differences that make your relationship uniquely yours—and, ultimately, make your love stronger than ever before.

Chapter 2

Brains Wired to Wander

How ADHD, Autism, and Other Neurotypes Affect Love, Intimacy, and Routine

The ability to understand, adjust to, and support one another's unique cognitive and emotional needs is often the key to building a long-lasting, loving partnership. However, for those who are neurodivergent, particularly those with conditions like ADHD, autism, and other neurotypes, the experience of love and intimacy is not always straightforward. These individuals may possess a distinct way of thinking, processing emotions, and experiencing the world around them. While neurodivergence can offer remarkable strengths and perspectives, it also brings challenges that can impact love, intimacy, and the smooth running of day-to-day routines.

In this chapter, we'll delve into the various relationship-relevant symptoms that arise from conditions such as ADHD, autism, and other neurotypes, including hyperfocus, overstimulation, executive dysfunction, and masking. We'll also explore how these traits shape the dynamics of love and intimacy in relationships, and how partners can develop strategies to navigate them in a way that fosters mutual understanding, respect, and connection. At the heart of this exploration is a powerful reframing of what it means to be "distracted" or "inconsistent"—concepts that, when viewed through the lens of neurodivergence, take on entirely new meanings.

Relationship-Relevant Symptoms: Hyperfocus, Overstimulation, Executive Dysfunction, Masking

Understanding the common symptoms associated with neurodivergence is key to understanding how these traits influence relationships. While each person's experience with neurodivergence is unique, several common traits tend to affect relationships in profound ways. These traits include hyperfocus, overstimulation, executive dysfunction, and masking.

1. **Hyperfocus**: Hyperfocus is a symptom most commonly associated with ADHD, though it can also be present in other neurotypes, including autism. Hyperfocus refers to a state of intense concentration on a task or activity to the point where everything else fades into the background. In a relationship, this trait can be both a gift and a challenge. On the one hand, hyperfocus can lead to remarkable productivity and creative output. However, it can also cause the neurodivergent partner to become completely absorbed in a project, neglecting the needs or presence of their partner. This can result in feelings of isolation, neglect, or frustration for the partner who feels "left out" or "unseen."

   o **Navigating hyperfocus**: The key to navigating hyperfocus in relationships is mutual understanding. A neurodivergent partner may not intentionally ignore their loved one, but rather may become so absorbed in their work or hobby that they lose track of time. It's essential for the neurotypical partner to understand that hyperfocus is a neurological trait, not a reflection of a lack of care. Conversely, the neurodivergent partner should learn to check in with their partner regularly and set intentional reminders to balance time spent on personal tasks with time devoted to the relationship.

2. **Overstimulation**: Neurodivergent individuals, particularly those with autism, often experience overstimulation in environments that may seem ordinary to neurotypical individuals. Overstimulation can occur in noisy or crowded spaces, during intense emotional conversations, or when faced with an overwhelming amount of sensory input. This can lead to meltdowns, withdrawal, or irritability. In relationships, overstimulation can create tension when one partner feels that their neurodivergent counterpart is being distant or irritable without clear reason.

   o **Navigating overstimulation**: Partners must work together to create an environment that minimizes overstimulation triggers. This may mean taking breaks during intense social events, finding quieter spaces to communicate, or establishing clear signals that one partner is feeling overwhelmed and needs space. Understanding that overstimulation is a genuine physical and emotional reaction can help both partners create a safe and supportive space for managing it.

3. **Executive Dysfunction**: Executive dysfunction refers to difficulties with organizing, planning, and completing tasks. It's a hallmark of ADHD and can also be present in other neurodivergent conditions. In relationships, this may manifest as a partner struggling to follow through on promises, meet deadlines, or handle routine responsibilities like household chores or planning. The neurotypical partner may interpret this as laziness, irresponsibility, or neglect. However, for the neurodivergent partner, executive dysfunction can feel like a constant battle with the brain to complete even the most basic tasks.

   o **Navigating executive dysfunction**: The key to managing executive dysfunction in relationships is developing clear structures, routines, and accountability systems. It may help to break tasks down into smaller, more manageable steps or use external reminders (such as alarms or to-do lists) to keep track of responsibilities. Additionally, neurotypical partners should recognize that the neurodivergent individual's difficulties are not intentional or due to lack of effort, but rather a cognitive challenge that requires support and understanding.

4. **Masking**: Masking refers to the coping mechanism used by many neurodivergent individuals, particularly those with autism, where

they consciously or unconsciously suppress their natural traits and behaviors in order to fit in with societal expectations. In relationships, masking can lead to a feeling of emotional disconnection, as the neurodivergent partner may struggle to express their true feelings, needs, and desires. Masking can also cause a partner to feel like they are not getting an authentic version of their loved one, which can lead to confusion, frustration, and emotional strain.

   o **Navigating masking**: The best way to navigate masking in relationships is to create a safe space where both partners can be their authentic selves. The neurodivergent individual should feel empowered to express themselves without fear of judgment, while the neurotypical partner should practice radical empathy and avoid putting pressure on the neurodivergent partner to "fit in" or conform. Open, honest communication about what is authentic versus what is "masked" can be incredibly liberating for both partners.

The Difference Between Being Distracted and Being Differently Focused

One of the most common misconceptions about neurodivergence is that individuals with conditions like ADHD are simply "distracted." In reality, what often appears as distraction is a different way of focusing attention. Neurodivergent individuals often struggle to control where their attention goes, but that doesn't mean they lack focus altogether. It's just that their focus may not always align with what others deem important or worthy of attention at a given moment.

For example, a neurodivergent partner might be deeply absorbed in a project that feels incredibly important to them, while the other partner might feel neglected because the task at hand is not a shared priority. It's not that the neurodivergent individual is distracted or uninterested in their partner—it's that their brain is wired to focus intensely on something that might seem trivial to others.

In relationships, this "differently focused" attention requires understanding and compromise. Neurodivergent individuals can work on honing their focus when it's necessary for the relationship, while their neurotypical partners can learn to appreciate that different focus doesn't mean a lack of care or love.

Navigating Routines, Rituals, and Change

Routines and rituals are the foundation of many relationships. Whether it's a weekly date night, a morning coffee ritual, or simply the way chores are divided, routines help maintain stability and provide a sense of shared purpose. However, for neurodivergent individuals, routines can either be a source of comfort or a source of frustration.

For example, individuals with autism may find comfort in predictability, while those with ADHD may struggle with the monotony of repetitive routines. In either case, change—whether it's a change in schedule, a shift in plans, or an unexpected event—can create stress and anxiety.

- **Navigating routines and change**: The key to managing routines and change in a neurodivergent relationship is flexibility and open communication. Neurodivergent individuals may benefit from a structured routine but may also need flexibility to accommodate their fluctuating energy levels, moods, or cognitive states. On the other hand, neurotypical partners may need to accept that spontaneity or last-minute changes may be more challenging for their neurodivergent counterpart. Working together to find a balance that works for both individuals is essential. Flexibility in adapting routines while maintaining a sense of stability can strengthen the relationship and reduce conflict around change.

Why Some Neurodivergent People Struggle with Consistency—and How to Reframe It

Consistency is often seen as an ideal in relationships. We expect our partners to consistently show up, keep promises, and adhere to routines. However, for neurodivergent individuals, consistency can be one of the most difficult challenges they face. Executive dysfunction, emotional regulation difficulties, and sensory overload can make it difficult to maintain the consistency that is often expected in relationships.

But rather than viewing inconsistency as a flaw or personal failing, it's important to reframe it as a challenge to be addressed collaboratively. Neurodivergent individuals often need additional support, structure, and understanding to maintain consistency in their actions. This might involve breaking tasks into smaller steps, using reminders, or creating systems of accountability that align with their cognitive style.

For neurotypical partners, reframing inconsistency means recognizing that their neurodivergent loved one's struggle is not a reflection of their love or commitment, but rather a cognitive challenge that can be addressed with patience and support. Embracing inconsistency as a natural part of neurodivergence allows both partners to approach challenges with greater compassion and understanding.

Conclusion

In relationships where neurodivergence is present, love, intimacy, and routine take on different meanings. The symptoms of hyperfocus, overstimulation, executive dysfunction, and masking all contribute to a unique dynamic that requires both partners to approach each other with radical empathy, curiosity, and flexibility. By reframing common challenges like distraction, inconsistency, and the difficulties with routines, neurodivergent couples can build a deeper, more meaningful connection that celebrates their differences and embraces their strengths.

Ultimately, love in the neurospicy lane is about accepting and understanding the ways in which our brains are wired to wander. It's not about fixing each other or conforming to societal expectations; it's about creating a relationship that works for both individuals, where love can flourish in all its beautifully unpredictable forms.

Chapter 3

The Sensory Spectrum of Affection

When Touch, Tone, and Time Mean Different Things

In any relationship, affection is a key ingredient—whether expressed through words, touch, or shared moments of connection. But for neurodivergent individuals, particularly those with sensory sensitivities, affection doesn't always look the same. Sensory experiences can shape how love is perceived and expressed, making the dynamics of intimacy unique in neurodiverse relationships. For individuals with autism, ADHD, or other neurotypes, touch, tone, and time may carry different meanings, intensities, and implications than they do for neurotypical individuals. Sensory sensitivities can affect everything from how affection is given to how it is received, and what one partner might find comforting or enjoyable, the other might find overwhelming or unbearable.

This chapter will delve into the sensory spectrum of affection, exploring how sensory sensitivities influence intimacy and daily interactions. We will look at the importance of creating safe sensory environments together, and how partners can better understand and support each other during sensory experiences like stimming, shutdowns, and meltdowns. Additionally, we'll explore the relationship between love languages and sensory preferences, highlighting how the two intersect in neurodivergent relationships. By the end of this chapter, readers will gain a deeper understanding of how to navigate affection in a way that accommodates both partners' sensory needs, fostering a loving and safe space for connection.

Sensory Sensitivities and How They Affect Intimacy and Daily Interactions

Sensory sensitivities are a hallmark of many neurodivergent conditions, particularly autism spectrum disorder (ASD), ADHD, and sensory processing disorder (SPD). These sensitivities refer to the heightened or diminished response to sensory stimuli—such as touch, sound, light, taste, or smell—that a neurodivergent person might experience. In relationships, these sensitivities can greatly influence how affection is experienced and how intimacy is shared.

For example, a person on the autism spectrum might have a heightened sensitivity to touch, meaning that physical contact such as a hug, kiss, or even a hand on the shoulder could feel uncomfortable, overstimulating, or even painful. On the other hand, someone with ADHD might have a high threshold for sensory input and seek out more intense forms of touch or affection, sometimes misreading the partner's cues in the process.

In daily interactions, these differences can manifest in seemingly mundane moments, like sitting too close together, loud noises, or bright lights. For the neurodivergent partner, these sensory experiences may cause discomfort, anxiety, or irritability. For the neurotypical partner, these behaviors might be confusing, leading to misunderstandings about their partner's level of affection or emotional availability. It's crucial for both partners to understand that these reactions are not a reflection of the relationship but a manifestation of sensory sensitivities.

Creating mutual awareness of each other's sensory sensitivities is essential. Understanding that sensory inputs such as sounds, textures, or lighting can have a profound impact on intimacy and emotional connection will help both partners approach affection in a more empathetic and supportive manner.

Creating Safe Sensory Environments Together

A key aspect of navigating sensory sensitivities in relationships is the creation of a safe sensory environment—an environment where both partners feel comfortable, secure, and able to connect without sensory overload. A safe sensory environment is one where sensory stimuli are tailored to accommodate the needs of both partners, promoting relaxation and reducing anxiety or overstimulation.

For neurodivergent individuals, this might mean setting up specific areas of the home that are quiet, dimly lit, and free from loud noises. It could involve creating boundaries around certain types of physical contact, such as hugs or touches, by asking for consent before initiating them. These small adjustments can significantly impact how neurodivergent partners experience intimacy and affection.

Additionally, safe sensory environments require open communication. Partners need to discuss their sensory needs and establish a shared understanding of what is comfortable and what is overwhelming. For instance, a partner who is sensitive to loud noises might need to set up a quiet space for relaxation or communication, while a partner who enjoys sensory input may want more dynamic environments. Being flexible and willing to adjust spaces, routines, and activities to accommodate each other's needs fosters an environment of care and consideration.

This mutual effort to create a safe sensory environment is a crucial act of love and support. It demonstrates the commitment of both partners to prioritize each other's comfort, security, and emotional well-being. In doing so, it allows for greater emotional and physical connection without the interference of sensory discomfort or overload.

Understanding Stimming, Shutdowns, and Meltdowns Through a Partner's Lens

Stimming, shutdowns, and meltdowns are behaviors commonly associated with neurodivergent individuals, particularly those on the autism spectrum. While these behaviors are often seen as manifestations of sensory overload or emotional dysregulation, they can deeply affect relationships if not understood or managed properly. In this section, we'll explore each of these behaviors and discuss how they affect intimacy and communication between partners.

1. **Stimming**: Stimming, short for self-stimulatory behavior, refers to repetitive physical movements or sounds that a neurodivergent individual engages in to self-regulate, reduce anxiety, or manage overwhelming sensory input. Examples of stimming include hand-flapping, rocking, repeating certain phrases, or tapping objects. While stimming is often misunderstood as a sign of

anxiety or discomfort, it's actually a coping mechanism that helps individuals process their environment.

2. In relationships, stimming can be misinterpreted by neurotypical partners as strange or inappropriate. However, understanding that stimming is a self-soothing behavior can allow the neurotypical partner to view it with compassion. Instead of feeling frustrated or uncomfortable, they can support their partner by allowing them space to stim when needed, or by engaging in stimming behaviors together if they feel comfortable. This can foster a sense of intimacy and understanding, where both partners respect each other's needs for emotional regulation.

3. **Shutdowns**: A shutdown is a form of emotional or sensory overload where an individual becomes overwhelmed and withdraws into themselves, often becoming unresponsive or unable to communicate. This can be triggered by overstimulation, stress, or even the accumulation of multiple smaller sensory challenges throughout the day. Shutdowns can be difficult for neurotypical partners to understand, as it may appear that their loved one is "shutting them out" or "ignoring" them. In reality, the neurodivergent partner may be experiencing a temporary inability to process emotions or sensory input.

4. During a shutdown, it's crucial for the neurotypical partner to remain patient and non-judgmental. Instead of pressuring the neurodivergent individual to communicate or engage, it's

important to offer a calming presence, provide comfort without expectations, and allow time and space for recovery. Being sensitive to shutdowns and recognizing them as a form of self-preservation can help prevent miscommunication and emotional harm in the relationship.

5. **Meltdowns**: Meltdowns are often the result of overwhelming sensory input or an emotional buildup that causes an individual to become overwhelmed and unable to regulate their emotions. This can lead to outbursts of anger, frustration, or distress. Unlike tantrums, which are often seen as a way of getting attention or control, meltdowns are involuntary reactions to sensory overload and emotional exhaustion.

6. For partners witnessing a meltdown, it can be emotionally difficult and confusing. However, understanding that meltdowns are not the result of willful behavior but a natural reaction to overwhelming circumstances can help. In these moments, it's important for the neurotypical partner to offer support in a calm, non-confrontational way. Providing a quiet space, removing sensory triggers, or simply being present without attempting to fix the situation can help the neurodivergent partner regain control and feel supported.

7. Recognizing that meltdowns are a form of communication is key. They signal that something is wrong—whether it's sensory overload, emotional dysregulation, or anxiety—and require patience and understanding, not reprimand or frustration.

Love Languages vs. Sensory Preferences

When it comes to expressing love, many people are familiar with the concept of love languages—acts of service, words of affirmation, receiving gifts, quality time, and physical touch. For neurodivergent individuals, love languages may take on different meanings, and preferences for how love is expressed and received can be influenced by sensory sensitivities.

For instance, a neurodivergent person with heightened tactile sensitivities might have a love language of "words of affirmation" rather than "physical touch," even though physical touch is typically seen as a universally popular love language. Similarly, a partner with autism may struggle with loud, boisterous displays of affection or public gestures but may deeply appreciate quiet acts of service or moments of calm, focused attention.

The key here is understanding that while love languages provide a helpful framework for expressing love, sensory preferences add an additional layer that needs to be considered. This means recognizing how certain love languages—especially physical touch—might not be universally comfortable or desirable for neurodivergent individuals.

The most important thing in neurodivergent relationships is to communicate openly about sensory preferences and find ways to express affection in ways that are comfortable for both partners. Sometimes, this might mean adapting or combining love languages to create a more sensory-friendly way of connecting.

For example, instead of physical touch, a neurodivergent partner may prefer a gentle gesture like holding hands in a way that respects their sensory needs, or they may feel loved through small acts of service, such as preparing their favorite meal or planning a quiet activity. Partners should be open to adapting their understanding of love languages to incorporate sensory needs, ensuring that love is felt deeply and consistently in the relationship.

Conclusion

Sensory sensitivities are an integral part of neurodivergent relationships. By acknowledging and addressing how touch, tone, and time impact intimacy and daily interactions, couples can create stronger, more resilient bonds. Creating safe sensory environments, understanding behaviors like stimming, shutdowns, and meltdowns, and recognizing the intersection between love languages and sensory preferences all contribute to fostering deeper emotional and physical connections.

By embracing the sensory spectrum of affection with empathy and understanding, both partners can feel more loved, supported, and valued. This chapter serves as a guide to navigating the complexities of sensory sensitivities, helping couples build a relationship that is not only supportive but also attuned to the unique needs of each individual. Love, after all, is about finding harmony and connection, even in the most intricate and nuanced experiences of affection.

Chapter 4

Communication, but Make It Neurodivergent-Friendly

How to Talk So Your Brain Can Hear It

Communication is the cornerstone of any healthy relationship. It's how we connect, express our feelings, share our needs, and resolve conflicts. For neurodivergent individuals—those with conditions like autism, ADHD, dyslexia, and other neurotypes—traditional methods of communication often don't align with the way their brains process and interpret information. What may seem like a simple conversation or a harmless joke to a neurotypical person can be confusing, frustrating, or even overwhelming to someone who is neurodivergent. For instance, the nuances of sarcasm, the subtle cues in tone, or the implied meaning in a conversation can be easily missed or misinterpreted. At the same time, neurodivergent individuals often have their own unique communication styles that might be misunderstood by neurotypical partners, friends, or family members.

In this chapter, we'll explore how communication between neurodivergent and neurotypical individuals can be improved, starting with an understanding of why certain communication styles can cause friction. We'll look at the importance of using literal language, directness, and clarifying questions as tools to ensure both partners are truly hearing each other. We'll also address how to avoid common neurotypical assumptions like relying on tone, sarcasm, or subtext. By incorporating scripts, structure, and visual communication tools, both neurodivergent and neurotypical partners can create a clearer, more effective communication system. Additionally, we'll examine conflict resolution techniques tailored to neurodivergent thinkers, which help minimize misunderstandings and foster a sense of collaboration in the face of disagreements.

The Art of Literal Language, Directness, and Clarifying Questions

One of the most fundamental challenges in communication for neurodivergent individuals is interpreting language in a literal way. While neurotypical individuals may rely on tone, body language, and contextual clues to understand the full meaning of a statement, neurodivergent individuals often process language more literally, without picking up on the subtleties that are so easily communicated by tone or subtext. This difference can lead to significant misunderstandings in relationships.

For example, a neurotypical person may say, "I'm so hungry, I could eat a horse," using humor and exaggeration to express their desire for food. However, a neurodivergent partner may take this statement literally, interpreting it as an odd, possibly even alarming desire to consume a horse. This kind of literal interpretation can create confusion, frustration, or even anxiety for the neurodivergent individual, especially if the intent behind the words was not understood correctly.

Literal language serves as a solution to this challenge. Neurodivergent individuals often find it easier to understand language when it is clear, unambiguous, and devoid of figurative speech or implied meaning. When communicating with a neurodivergent partner, it's important to express thoughts and emotions directly, using straightforward language. For example, instead of saying, "I'm feeling a little under the weather," one might say, "I am not feeling well right now, and I need rest."

Similarly, directness in communication is key. Neurodivergent individuals may struggle with reading between the lines or understanding hints, so offering a direct approach—whether discussing needs, feelings, or preferences—can minimize confusion. It's also essential to keep the tone neutral and clear, avoiding emotional undertones that might be difficult for the neurodivergent partner to pick up on.

One practical tool for improving communication is clarifying questions. These questions are designed to check understanding and ensure that both partners are on the same page. Rather than assuming what the other person means, clarifying questions provide an opportunity for each partner to voice their perspective and confirm their understanding. Examples include:

- "What do you mean when you say that?"

- "Can you explain that a little more clearly?"

- "Are you feeling [emotion]? Is that right?"

By fostering an open dialogue through these clarifying questions, both neurodivergent and neurotypical individuals can better understand each other's thoughts, feelings, and intentions. This approach not only minimizes misunderstandings but also strengthens the relationship by promoting a culture of mutual respect and understanding.

Avoiding Neurotypical Assumptions: Hints, Tone, Sarcasm, and Subtext

In neurotypical communication, it's common to rely on hints, tone, sarcasm, and subtext to convey meaning beyond the literal words. For example, if a partner says, "That's just great!" with an exaggerated, irritated tone, the listener understands that the speaker is not actually pleased but is instead frustrated. Similarly, if someone says, "I'm fine," but the tone of voice suggests otherwise, a neurotypical person may pick up on the implied meaning—that the person is not truly fine.

However, for neurodivergent individuals, these forms of indirect communication can be incredibly confusing. The emphasis on tone and subtext might be missed entirely, leading to significant misinterpretations. The neurodivergent partner might believe the words at face value or struggle to decipher the hidden message embedded in the tone or body language.

To bridge this gap, it's crucial for neurotypical partners to avoid relying on tone, sarcasm, or subtext when communicating with their neurodivergent loved one. Instead, messages should be clear, explicit, and direct. Rather than using sarcasm or indirect phrasing, it's better to say exactly what you mean. For instance, instead of saying, "Oh, great, another surprise," which could be interpreted as sarcasm, it would be more effective to say, "I'm feeling frustrated by this unexpected situation."

In addition, explicit communication can also include nonverbal cues. Neurodivergent individuals may struggle to pick up on body language or facial expressions, so it's important to offer direct eye contact and appropriate gestures when necessary to supplement verbal communication. This can help prevent misreading the emotional tone of a conversation and ensure both partners feel heard and understood.

For neurotypical partners, understanding that their neurodivergent loved one may not pick up on these nuances is key. Moving away from the use of indirect communication will promote a healthier, more transparent dialogue, where both partners feel confident in expressing themselves.

Scripts, Structure, and Visual Communication Tools That Help

While direct verbal communication is important, some neurodivergent individuals may still benefit from additional forms of communication that provide more structure and clarity. Scripts, visual tools, and structured communication can be incredibly helpful in facilitating more effective conversations, especially when discussing complex topics or navigating challenging emotional situations.

Communication scripts provide a structured way of approaching sensitive conversations. These scripts might include specific phrases or formats that help both partners understand the conversation's flow and ensure that nothing important is left unsaid. For example, when discussing a sensitive issue, one might use a script such as:

1. "I want to talk about [issue]."

2. "This is how I feel about it: [emotion]."

3. "This is what I need from you: [request]."

4. "How do you feel about this?"

These structured formats help both partners stay on track, avoid misunderstandings, and express themselves clearly. Using scripts can also reduce the anxiety or overwhelm that often accompanies difficult conversations, providing both partners with a roadmap for navigating complex topics.

Visual communication tools can also be invaluable, especially for neurodivergent individuals who struggle with processing verbal information alone. Tools such as charts, graphs, written notes, and illustrations can help clarify complex ideas and ensure both partners are on the same page. For instance, using a visual schedule can help neurodivergent individuals track daily routines or important tasks, while visual aids like emotive charts or pictorial representations can help express feelings or intentions when words might be difficult to convey.

Other tools, like written reminders, whiteboards, or shared digital calendars, can help both partners keep track of commitments, important dates, and ongoing conversations. By using visual tools in conjunction with verbal communication, both neurodivergent and neurotypical individuals can ensure that information is being processed and retained in a way that makes sense for both parties.

Conflict Resolution Techniques Tailored for Neurodivergent Thinkers

Conflicts are an inevitable part of any relationship, but when neurodivergent individuals are involved, the way conflicts are approached and resolved requires additional consideration. The traditional conflict resolution strategies—such as focusing on emotions, using indirect language, or expecting immediate resolution—may not work well for neurodivergent individuals who process emotions differently, struggle with emotional regulation, or have difficulty understanding abstract concepts.

Here are several conflict resolution techniques that are tailored for neurodivergent thinkers:

1. **Give Time and Space**: Neurodivergent individuals, especially those on the autism spectrum, may need time to process information before engaging in a conflict resolution discussion. Rather than expecting an immediate response, allow the person to take a break and return to the conversation when they're ready. This helps prevent emotional overwhelm and ensures that both partners can approach the conversation with clarity.

2. **Use Structured Problem-Solving**: Instead of diving straight into emotions during a conflict, break the issue down into clear, manageable steps. Define the problem, discuss possible

solutions, and decide on an action plan. For example, instead of saying, "We always fight about this!" you might start with, "There's an issue with [specific action]. Let's talk about how we can fix it."

3. **Avoid Ambiguity**: Use literal and direct language when resolving conflicts. Instead of saying, "I feel like you never listen to me," say, "I feel unheard when you don't respond to me in the moment." This reduces the chance for misinterpretation and provides clear direction for the conversation.

4. **Acknowledge Sensory Overload**: If one partner is feeling overwhelmed due to sensory sensitivities, acknowledge that sensory overload can exacerbate conflicts. Offer a quiet, calm space where both partners can take a step back before resuming the discussion.

5. **Use Written Communication**: For some neurodivergent individuals, written communication can be more effective than verbal communication during conflicts. This allows both partners to express themselves clearly and allows time for thoughtful responses.

By using these neurodivergent-friendly conflict resolution techniques, couples can navigate disagreements with greater understanding and empathy. These strategies promote calm, productive conversations and prevent conflicts from escalating unnecessarily.

Conclusion

Communication is the foundation of any relationship, and in neurodivergent relationships, it's essential to adapt communication strategies to ensure that both partners are truly hearing each other. By embracing literal language, directness, and clarifying questions, neurodivergent and neurotypical partners can create a clearer, more open dialogue. Avoiding assumptions about tone, sarcasm, and subtext, and using visual tools and structured communication, can further enhance understanding and reduce misunderstandings. Finally, implementing conflict resolution techniques tailored for neurodivergent thinkers can help navigate challenges in a way that promotes collaboration, empathy, and respect.

At the heart of neurodivergent-friendly communication is the recognition that everyone processes information differently. By fostering an environment where both partners feel heard, understood, and respected, communication becomes not just an exchange of words but a means of connection that strengthens the relationship.

Chapter 5

Emotions on Different Frequencies

Dysregulation, Empathy, and Emotional Misfires

Emotions are powerful forces that shape our experiences, guide our decisions, and drive our relationships. They help us connect with others and navigate the ups and downs of daily life. But for neurodivergent individuals—those with conditions like autism, ADHD, and other neurotypes—emotions can be experienced in unique and sometimes intense ways. Emotional regulation, the ability to manage and respond to emotional experiences in a balanced way, can be particularly challenging. For some neurodivergent individuals, emotions may be overwhelming, leading to dysregulation, emotional outbursts, or withdrawal. For others, emotional suppression may become a coping mechanism, leaving their partners feeling disconnected or unsure of what's truly going on beneath the surface.

In this chapter, we'll explore the complex landscape of emotions in neurodivergent relationships, focusing on emotional regulation versus suppression, why some neurodivergent individuals may appear "detached" or "too intense," and how partners can better understand each other's emotional styles and triggers. We'll also discuss how to navigate challenging emotional situations, including panic attacks, emotional shutdowns, or feelings of rejection, with empathy and understanding. By developing a deeper awareness of emotional experiences from both partners' perspectives, couples can build stronger, more compassionate relationships that honor both the differences and the common ground they share.

Emotional Regulation vs. Emotional Suppression

Emotional regulation refers to the ability to manage and adjust one's emotional responses to various situations. It involves recognizing and understanding one's emotions, expressing them appropriately, and coping with them in healthy ways. For neurodivergent individuals, emotional regulation can be a particularly challenging skill to master. For example, individuals with ADHD may experience rapid emotional shifts, where excitement or frustration can escalate quickly. Similarly, people with autism may have difficulty understanding or expressing their emotions, leading to feelings of being overwhelmed or misunderstood.

When emotional regulation is difficult, it can lead to emotional dysregulation—a state where emotions become unmanageable or disproportionately intense. This can manifest as emotional outbursts, irritability, or feelings of being "out of control." Emotional dysregulation often occurs in response to sensory overload, social challenges, or overwhelming situations, where the individual is unable to process their feelings in a calm and balanced way. For neurodivergent individuals, this can create moments of intense emotional responses that seem disproportionate to others, leading to misunderstandings in relationships.

On the other hand, emotional suppression is a coping mechanism in which neurodivergent individuals try to hide or avoid their emotions to prevent them from overwhelming themselves or others. Suppression can occur as a result of feeling like their emotions are too intense or too difficult to express, or because they fear judgment or rejection. For example, someone with autism might suppress their emotions in social settings to avoid standing out or causing discomfort, even if they are experiencing distress internally. Similarly, a neurodivergent partner with ADHD might suppress their emotions when they feel like they are being judged for their emotional responses.

The difference between emotional regulation and emotional suppression is subtle but important. Regulation involves acknowledging and working through emotions, while suppression involves denying or hiding them. Emotional suppression, while it may seem like a coping strategy in the short term, can lead to long-term consequences like emotional burnout, resentment, or a sense of disconnection in relationships.

To help a neurodivergent partner, it's crucial to create an environment where emotional regulation can thrive. This means acknowledging that emotional dysregulation is not a sign of weakness, but a natural response to intense emotions or overwhelming situations. Encouraging emotional expression and providing support through active listening, validation, and patience can help neurodivergent individuals navigate their emotions in healthy ways, rather than resorting to suppression.

Why Some Neurodivergent People Seem "Detached" or "Too Intense"

Emotions are often expressed in different ways depending on one's neurotype. Neurodivergent individuals may experience emotions more intensely or may have difficulty expressing them in socially accepted ways, leading to perceptions of being "detached" or "too intense." Understanding these differences is key to building empathy in relationships.

1. **Detached**: For some neurodivergent individuals, particularly those on the autism spectrum, emotional expression may seem limited or distant. This can manifest in a lack of visible emotional reactions, reduced eye contact, or a preference for solitary activities. These behaviors can be misunderstood by neurotypical partners as emotional detachment or a lack of interest. However, for many neurodivergent individuals, this "detachment" is not a lack of emotion, but rather a difference in how emotions are expressed or processed.

    o   For instance, an individual with autism may experience emotions deeply but find it difficult to express those feelings outwardly. They may not display the same outward signs of affection or empathy that their neurotypical partner expects, but this does not mean they are not experiencing love or care. Their emotional connection may be communicated through actions rather than words or physical expressions.

o How to Partner with the "Detached" Partner: The key to connecting with someone who appears detached is patience and understanding. Instead of assuming that emotional distance equates to a lack of love or connection, it's important to ask the neurodivergent partner about their emotional experience and how they prefer to express or process their feelings. Engaging in direct and non-judgmental communication can help bridge the gap and deepen emotional connection.

2. **Too Intense**: On the flip side, some neurodivergent individuals, particularly those with ADHD or emotional sensitivity, may experience emotions more intensely than their neurotypical counterparts. This heightened emotional experience can result in emotional outbursts, where a seemingly small issue is met with disproportionate emotional reactions, such as frustration, anger, or excitement. These intense emotions can sometimes overwhelm neurotypical partners, leading to perceptions of the neurodivergent individual being "too much" or "overreacting."

o For example, a person with ADHD might have difficulty managing frustration, resulting in loud expressions of anger over relatively minor issues. Likewise, an individual with high emotional sensitivity may cry or become overwhelmed during seemingly neutral or insignificant moments. This intensity, while deeply felt, can be hard for neurotypical partners to process, especially if they don't understand the neurodivergent partner's emotional experience.

○ How to Partner with the "Too Intense" Partner: When dealing with an emotionally intense neurodivergent partner, it's essential to approach the situation with empathy and compassion. Rather than dismissing their emotional responses as overreactions, recognize that their feelings are valid and that the intensity of their emotions may stem from sensory overload, emotional regulation challenges, or unprocessed feelings. Offer reassurance, space, and strategies to help them manage their emotional response in a constructive way.

Identifying Your Emotional Styles and Triggers

Every person has their own emotional style, or the way in which they process, express, and regulate their emotions. For neurodivergent individuals, these emotional styles are often shaped by their neurological makeup. Some individuals may be highly sensitive to emotions and find it difficult to manage intense feelings, while others may struggle to identify or express their emotions clearly.

Identifying emotional styles is an important step in creating a strong emotional connection in a relationship. By understanding how both partners experience and express emotions, couples can better navigate emotional challenges and foster a deeper sense of understanding. Here are some questions to help identify emotional styles:

- How do I react when I feel overwhelmed or stressed?

- Do I prefer to be alone when I'm upset, or do I want support?

- How do I express affection—verbally, physically, or through actions?

- What emotions do I find most difficult to express, and why?

- How do I cope with feelings of anger, sadness, or anxiety?

For neurodivergent individuals, identifying emotional triggers is equally important. Emotional triggers are situations, comments, or experiences that cause intense emotional reactions, often linked to past experiences or unmet needs. Common triggers for neurodivergent individuals might include:

- **Sensory overload**: Bright lights, loud noises, or crowded spaces can trigger emotional distress.

- **Misunderstandings**: Not being understood or having emotions dismissed can lead to frustration and anger.

- **Uncertainty**: Unclear expectations or unpredictable situations can create anxiety.

- **Rejection or perceived rejection**: Neurodivergent individuals may be particularly sensitive to rejection, real or imagined.

Once emotional triggers are identified, both partners can work together to minimize or address them. This might involve creating sensory-friendly environments, communicating more clearly about expectations, or discussing ways to handle difficult emotional situations proactively.

Partnering Through Panic, Shutdowns, or Rejections

Emotional dysregulation in neurodivergent individuals can sometimes lead to panic attacks, shutdowns, or feelings of rejection. These experiences are often misunderstood by neurotypical partners, who may not know how to respond or may feel helpless in the face of their partner's emotional overwhelm.

1. **Panic Attacks**: A panic attack is an intense, overwhelming emotional experience characterized by physical symptoms such as rapid heart rate, shortness of breath, dizziness, and a sense of impending doom. Panic attacks are common in individuals with anxiety, ADHD, and other neurotypes, and they can arise suddenly in response to stress, sensory overload, or an emotional trigger.

    o   **How to Partner Through Panic**: During a panic attack, the neurotypical partner should focus on offering calm, grounding support. This can include offering physical comfort (if the neurodivergent partner is comfortable with touch), guiding them through deep breathing exercises, or simply providing a safe, quiet space to recover.

2. **Shutdowns**: A shutdown occurs when an individual becomes overwhelmed to the point of withdrawing emotionally and physically. This often happens in response to sensory overload, anxiety, or emotional exhaustion. The person may appear "shut down" or unresponsive.

○ **How to Partner Through Shutdowns**: When a partner is experiencing a shutdown, it's important to offer space without taking it personally. Avoid pressuring them to communicate or engage before they are ready. Instead, reassure them that it's okay to take time for themselves and that you're there when they're ready to talk.

3. **Rejection Sensitivity**: Many neurodivergent individuals experience rejection sensitivity, which means they have an exaggerated emotional response to perceived rejection or criticism. This can result in heightened emotional reactions, even to small or unintentional slights.

○ **How to Partner Through Rejection Sensitivity**: Understanding that rejection sensitivity is a real emotional experience can help mitigate misunderstandings. Neurotypical partners should be mindful of their tone and language, especially during disagreements. Reassuring words, gentle validation, and clear communication about intentions can help alleviate the emotional weight of perceived rejection.

Conclusion

Emotions in neurodivergent relationships are complex and multifaceted. Dysregulation, emotional intensity, and suppression can all play a significant role in how love is expressed and experienced. By understanding the differences in emotional regulation, recognizing the impact of emotional triggers, and learning how to partner through panic, shutdowns, and rejection sensitivity, couples can build stronger, more empathetic connections.

The key to navigating emotional challenges in neurodivergent relationships lies in developing mutual understanding and compassion. By recognizing the unique emotional experiences of each partner, couples can work together to create an emotionally supportive environment that fosters trust, love, and emotional growth. Through empathy, open communication, and practical strategies, both partners can learn to navigate emotions on different frequencies and build a relationship that honors their individual needs and experiences.

Chapter 6

The Myth of the "Normal" Relationship

Letting Go of Neurotypical Love Templates

From movies to social media to traditional cultural narratives, society has long dictated a specific blueprint for romantic relationships—one that often follows a linear progression of courtship, deepening affection, commitment, and eventual stability. This "normal" relationship template, often centered around neurotypical patterns of communication, emotional regulation, and interaction, is deeply ingrained in our collective consciousness. For many couples, this template serves as the standard against which all relationships are measured. However, for neurodivergent individuals—those whose cognitive and emotional experiences differ from the neurotypical norm—this standard often does not apply.

The pressure to conform to these traditional expectations can be exhausting, isolating, and ultimately damaging to neurodivergent couples who do not fit neatly into this predefined box. Neurodivergent love, with its unique dynamics, doesn't always follow the prescribed path, and that's okay. In fact, it's not just okay—it can be revolutionary.

In this chapter, we will explore how neurodivergent love bends, blends, and breaks societal traditions. We will challenge the myth of the "normal" relationship, rethinking conventional expectations about romance, intimacy, and emotional connection. We will dive into the concept of nonlinear relationship growth, exploring what it looks like for neurodivergent couples and why it is perfectly acceptable to deviate from traditional timelines. Most importantly, we will embrace difference as design, not dysfunction, understanding that neurodivergent relationships offer valuable insights into how love can thrive when it is allowed to evolve outside of societal constraints.

Rethinking Societal Expectations of Romantic Relationships

From the moment we are born, we are inundated with cultural narratives about what love should look like. Whether it's fairy tales that promise "happily ever after" or contemporary rom-coms that depict love as a series of flawless encounters, society has long sold us a specific vision of romance. This vision, though beautiful on screen, is often out of touch with the diverse and complex nature of real-life relationships, particularly those between neurodivergent individuals.

Society tells us that relationships should progress in a linear fashion. You meet someone, you date, you fall in love, you move in together, you get married, and you build a life together. This narrative is romanticized, idealized, and often positioned as the "right" or "normal" way to experience love. However, for neurodivergent individuals, this traditional roadmap can feel restrictive, alienating, or even impossible to follow.

Neurodivergent couples may not experience romantic milestones in the same order or at the same pace as neurotypical couples. They may not express love in the same ways, nor do they necessarily operate within the same boundaries of emotional regulation and communication. Yet, because the dominant cultural narrative around relationships is based on a neurotypical template, neurodivergent couples can feel pressured to fit their experiences into a mold that doesn't reflect their reality.

It's time to rethink these societal expectations. Rather than measuring the success of a relationship by how well it adheres to a prescribed script, we need to acknowledge that love can be just as profound, authentic, and fulfilling when it does not follow the traditional narrative. By embracing a more inclusive, flexible view of relationships, we open the door to recognizing that every relationship—neurodivergent or neurotypical—has its own unique path, its own rhythm, and its own timeline.

How Neurodivergent Love Bends, Blends, and Breaks Traditions

Neurodivergent love often challenges conventional expectations, not because it is flawed or broken, but because it is fundamentally different. It bends, blends, and breaks traditions in ways that reflect the diverse experiences of those who live outside the neurotypical norm.

1. **Bending Traditions**: Neurodivergent couples may follow traditional relationship structures, but they bend them to fit their unique needs. For example, while traditional relationships might expect partners to share similar interests or spend a lot of time together, neurodivergent individuals may need more space to process their emotions or may have different sensory needs. A neurodivergent partner might find prolonged social interactions

50

draining, leading to the need for downtime or solitude. In these cases, love is still present, but it manifests in a way that accommodates individual needs for personal space, autonomy, and self-regulation.

- o **Example**: One partner might prefer quieter, less crowded settings, while the other enjoys socializing in larger groups. Instead of following the conventional expectation of doing everything together, the couple finds a balance—attending social events together for short periods or rotating who makes social plans based on comfort levels. Love is expressed not through proximity, but through mutual respect for each other's preferences.

2. **Blending Traditions**: In some neurodivergent relationships, elements of both neurotypical and neurodivergent relationship templates may be blended together. This blending allows each partner to bring their own emotional needs, communication styles, and coping strategies to the relationship, creating a new framework for connection. Neurodivergent couples often have to blend different ways of perceiving the world, processing emotions, and interpreting social cues.

- o **Example**: A neurodivergent partner with autism might have difficulty reading subtle emotional cues or understanding sarcasm, while the neurotypical partner might rely on these cues in communication. To blend their communication styles, the couple might establish clear, direct verbal communication rules—one where sarcasm and implied meaning are avoided, and straightforward, literal language is prioritized. This adaptation strengthens their bond by fostering clarity and reducing misunderstandings.

3. **Breaking Traditions**: Neurodivergent love often breaks traditions completely, leaving behind societal expectations of what relationships "should" look like. This is especially true in areas like commitment, communication, and emotional connection. Neurodivergent relationships may not follow traditional timelines for love, commitment, or marriage, nor do they necessarily subscribe to conventional ideas about gender roles, expectations, or shared responsibilities.

   o **Example**: A neurodivergent couple might not follow the conventional trajectory of dating, moving in together, and eventually getting married. Instead, they may prioritize living independently and building a partnership based on mutual respect and support, rather than societal milestones. The key to breaking traditions is to create a relationship model that honors both partners' neurodivergent needs and desires.

Breaking away from these traditions doesn't imply dysfunction; it simply means that love doesn't have to adhere to a single, standard narrative. Neurodivergent love is diverse and complex, and its beauty lies in the freedom to redefine what romance and connection mean on an individual level.

Nonlinear Relationship Growth: What It Looks Like and Why It's Okay

One of the most prominent features of neurodivergent relationships is nonlinear growth—a relationship trajectory that doesn't follow the conventional linear path from infatuation to commitment to long-term stability. For neurodivergent individuals, relationship growth may be slower, faster, or take unexpected twists and turns. This nonlinear growth is often misunderstood or judged as a sign of dysfunction. However, it is simply a reflection of the diverse ways in which individuals connect, communicate, and evolve together.

In a neurodivergent relationship, milestones may not happen in the "expected" order, and that's perfectly fine. A couple might experience periods of intense closeness followed by moments of emotional distance, not because their love is faltering, but because their individual emotional processes require time to adjust or recalibrate. These fluctuations are normal, especially for neurodivergent individuals who may need more time to process emotions or who experience sensory and emotional overload in different ways.

- **Example**: A couple may go through a phase of emotional detachment, where one or both partners withdraw to process personal emotions or external stressors. This might seem like a "breakup phase" from a neurotypical perspective, but in reality, this phase is an opportunity for each partner to reflect, recharge, and return to the relationship with new insights. The relationship doesn't fail—it simply grows in its own time and rhythm.

Nonlinear growth in a relationship allows for more flexibility and authenticity, as couples are not bound by rigid expectations. Instead, they can embrace the ebb and flow of their emotional connection, knowing that both the ups and downs are part of the larger journey of understanding, adaptation, and love.

Embracing Difference as Design—Not Dysfunction

Ultimately, the key to thriving in a neurodivergent relationship lies in embracing difference as design, not dysfunction. Society often views neurodivergence as a deviation from the norm—something that needs to be "fixed" or adjusted. In reality, neurodivergent relationships offer a chance to celebrate and design love in a way that works for both partners, honoring their unique neurological and emotional experiences.

Rather than seeing neurodivergent traits—whether it's a preference for routines, a different way of expressing emotions, or a unique communication style—as obstacles to love, they can be viewed as integral aspects of the relationship's design. These differences are what make the relationship distinct and valuable. Neurodivergent individuals bring creativity, depth, and new perspectives to relationships, and when these qualities are embraced, they can lead to stronger, more fulfilling connections.

In neurodivergent love, difference is not a problem to be solved; it is an opportunity to design a relationship that is authentic, adaptive, and deeply meaningful. The strength of neurodivergent relationships lies in their ability to defy the conventional templates of love, forging a path that is uniquely suited to the needs and desires of both partners.

Conclusion

The myth of the "normal" relationship is a product of societal expectations that fail to account for the diversity of human experiences. Neurodivergent love, with its ability to bend, blend, and break traditions, offers a refreshing alternative to the conventional relationship template. By letting go of the myth of the "normal" relationship, we open ourselves to the possibility of embracing love in all its forms—whether it follows a linear path, evolves nonlinearly, or defies traditional expectations entirely. In the end, what matters most is not adhering to a predefined script, but building a relationship that is authentic, adaptive, and tailored to the needs and experiences of both partners. Embracing difference as design allows neurodivergent couples to create a love story that is truly their own—one that is rich, dynamic, and deeply fulfilling.

Chapter 7

Attention, Affection, and the ADHD Rollercoaster

Navigating Hyperfocus, Inattention, and Intimacy

Love in an ADHD-affected relationship is anything but ordinary. It's a beautiful, chaotic, and exhilarating journey where attention, affection, and connection constantly shift, fluctuate, and morph. For partners in relationships where one (or both) individuals has ADHD, navigating intimacy and emotional bonds can feel like riding a rollercoaster—full of thrilling highs, unexpected dips, and plenty of loops. The ADHD experience—marked by hyperfocus, inattention, impulsivity, and emotional sensitivity—plays a profound role in how affection is expressed and experienced. It can either enhance the connection or cause tension depending on how both partners understand and navigate the challenges ADHD brings to their dynamic.

In this chapter, we'll dive deep into the unique emotional landscape of ADHD-affected relationships, addressing the phenomena of honeymoon hyperfocus, rejection sensitivity, and how ADHD affects intimacy. We'll discuss how relationships with ADHD partners can sometimes feel "hot and cold" or even "differently wired" due to the neurological factors at play. Finally, we'll explore how ADHD-related traits like time blindness and impulsivity can impact love, communication, and everyday interactions, offering insights into how to create balance and understanding despite the inherent challenges.

The "Honeymoon Hyperfocus" Effect and How It Can Shift

One of the most defining features of ADHD is hyperfocus—the ability to become intensely absorbed in an activity or object to the exclusion of everything else. While this trait can be a gift in some situations, such as during creative work or tasks that require deep concentration, it can also lead to challenges in romantic relationships.

The "honeymoon hyperfocus" effect is something many ADHD couples experience early in a relationship. At the start, the neurodivergent partner might become completely absorbed in their new partner, dedicating intense attention and affection to them. During this phase, the ADHD partner may feel deeply connected, constantly thinking about their loved one, texting or calling frequently, and prioritizing their partner above everything else. This intense focus feels like the "honeymoon phase" on steroids, with the relationship getting all of their emotional energy and attention.

However, as time goes on, this phase often shifts. The partner with ADHD might start to lose the intense focus they had during the honeymoon period. This shift can be jarring for both partners. For the ADHD individual, the initial intensity fades naturally as their attention moves to new interests or tasks that captivate them. For the non-ADHD partner, this can feel like a sudden withdrawal of affection or attention— leading to feelings of neglect or insecurity.

The key to navigating this shift is understanding that hyperfocus is not a reflection of love or lack of commitment, but rather a neurological trait that makes attention highly fluid. Partners in ADHD-affected relationships should be prepared for this cycle of intense focus followed by periods of distraction or disengagement. Open communication is crucial during these transitions to prevent misunderstandings and emotional wounds. Neurotypical partners should recognize that this shift is not a personal slight, and ADHD partners should make conscious efforts to maintain connection during periods of lower focus.

One strategy to manage this is by creating structured check-ins and mutual agreements about quality time. For example, scheduling regular dates, having a "connection time" each day, or even using reminders can help the ADHD partner stay engaged and present. These efforts make it clear that, while their focus may shift, their love and commitment to the relationship remain steadfast.

Understanding ADHD-Related Rejection Sensitivity (RSD)

Another emotional challenge in ADHD relationships is rejection sensitivity dysphoria (RSD)—a common and often painful experience for individuals with ADHD. RSD refers to an extreme emotional reaction to perceived rejection or criticism. For individuals with ADHD, even minor social cues, a misplaced comment, or an unintentional gesture can be interpreted as rejection, leading to intense emotional pain. This heightened sensitivity is due to the ADHD brain's unique way of processing emotions, where perceived rejection or failure is often amplified.

In relationships, RSD can manifest as disproportionate reactions to disagreements, misunderstandings, or even moments when the neurotypical partner is frustrated or upset. The ADHD partner may interpret these moments as signs of rejection, abandonment, or failure, even if this is not the intention of their loved one.

For the neurotypical partner, this behavior can be confusing and overwhelming. A seemingly small comment might trigger an emotional outburst or shutdown from the ADHD partner, leaving the neurotypical individual unsure of how to respond or fix the situation.

Managing RSD in a relationship requires compassion, patience, and a high level of emotional awareness. The neurotypical partner should understand that RSD is a real and painful experience, not just "overreacting" or "being too sensitive." Instead of dismissing the ADHD partner's emotional response, the neurotypical partner should validate their feelings and offer reassurance. It may help to create an emotional safety net, where both partners feel comfortable sharing their vulnerabilities without fear of judgment.

One important step in managing RSD is to set clear, supportive communication guidelines. Instead of vague comments or criticisms, try to be specific, kind, and constructive. For example, instead of saying, "You're always so disorganized," say, "I feel frustrated when things are left unfinished, and I'd appreciate it if we could find a way to keep things on track together." This type of clarity minimizes the risk of triggering RSD, while still addressing the issue at hand.

Intimacy in an ADHD-Affected Relationship: Hot, Cold, or Differently Wired

Intimacy in relationships affected by ADHD can often feel like a rollercoaster ride—sometimes hot, sometimes cold, and sometimes feeling like it's wired completely differently than what's expected. ADHD affects the way individuals process emotions, engage in physical affection, and sustain attention during intimate moments. As a result, intimacy can fluctuate, leaving both partners confused about the emotional connection.

The "hot" moments refer to those times when the ADHD partner is hyperfocused and emotionally engaged, leading to passionate, intense expressions of affection. This can include deep emotional connection, spontaneous affection, and a desire to be physically close. These moments are often the high points of the relationship, where both partners feel deeply connected and in sync.

The "cold" moments, however, are those times when the ADHD partner is distracted, unfocused, or disengaged. They may seem distant, uninterested, or preoccupied with other thoughts or tasks. This can be particularly challenging for the neurotypical partner, who may feel rejected or undervalued, even though the ADHD partner's lack of attention is not a reflection of their emotional investment.

The "differently wired" moments occur when intimacy is expressed in ways that are not conventionally recognized. For example, the ADHD partner may show love through acts of service, like planning a surprise date or fixing something around the house, rather than through verbal affirmations or physical touch. These differences can create a unique, sometimes perplexing intimacy dynamic in the relationship, but they also provide opportunities to redefine what love and affection mean for both partners.

To navigate these fluctuations, both partners should approach intimacy with flexibility and creativity. Instead of trying to conform to traditional ideas of romantic behavior, they can find their own unique ways of expressing affection. For example, the ADHD partner might set reminders to give their neurotypical partner attention during moments when they tend to get distracted, or the neurotypical partner might suggest ways to engage in intimacy that accommodate the ADHD partner's attention span.

Loving Someone with Time Blindness and Impulsivity

Two other key traits of ADHD—time blindness and impulsivity—can significantly impact intimacy and relationship dynamics. Time blindness refers to the difficulty individuals with ADHD have in perceiving the passage of time accurately. They may lose track of time, underestimating how long tasks take, or they may struggle with punctuality and meeting deadlines. This can be frustrating for the neurotypical partner, especially if they have a strong sense of time or value schedules and plans.

Impulsivity, on the other hand, manifests as spontaneous actions or decisions made without fully considering the consequences. This can range from making impromptu plans without consulting the partner to saying things in the heat of the moment without thinking through the impact. While impulsivity can lead to exciting, adventurous moments, it can also create tension, misunderstandings, and feelings of instability in the relationship.

Loving someone with time blindness and impulsivity requires understanding, patience, and the development of supportive strategies. For time blindness, couples can work together to create external systems to keep track of time, such as using shared calendars, setting alarms, or establishing routines that help the ADHD partner stay on track. For impulsivity, the neurotypical partner might offer gentle reminders or even introduce structured decision-making strategies, such as taking a pause before making big decisions.

It's essential to approach these traits with non-judgmental empathy. Instead of viewing time blindness and impulsivity as flaws or failures, recognize them as aspects of ADHD that require adaptation and support. When both partners are committed to understanding these challenges, they can create a relationship dynamic that is both accommodating and fulfilling.

Conclusion

Love in an ADHD-affected relationship is a dynamic, ever-evolving experience. From the honeymoon hyperfocus to the shifting tides of intimacy, ADHD creates a unique set of challenges and opportunities for connection. By understanding the impact of ADHD-related traits like rejection sensitivity, time blindness, and impulsivity, couples can navigate the rollercoaster of emotions and affection with empathy, patience, and creativity. The key is to recognize that ADHD is not a barrier to love, but a different way of experiencing and expressing it.

By embracing these differences, neurodivergent and neurotypical partners can find new ways to connect, communicate, and support each other. ADHD doesn't have to derail a relationship—it can lead to a deeper, more nuanced understanding of one another, fostering a love that is as rich, diverse, and unpredictable as the ADHD brain itself.

Chapter 8

When the Social Battery Dies

Social Needs, Alone Time, and Partnering Through Burnout

Every relationship requires a delicate balancing act—especially when it comes to social engagements and the inevitable need for alone time. For neurodivergent individuals, navigating this balance is often more challenging. Many neurodivergent individuals experience social situations differently, leading to unique needs for both social interaction and solitude. These needs can shift depending on the individual's neurotype, personality, and sensory processing, causing fluctuations in energy levels, mood, and capacity for socialization. For partners in a relationship where one or both individuals are neurodivergent, understanding the dynamics of social energy and managing moments of burnout is crucial for maintaining a healthy, supportive connection.

In this chapter, we will explore how the introvert-extrovert spectrum is often redefined by neurodivergence, diving into how social needs—whether for engagement or solitude—play a role in relationships. We'll also discuss strategies for managing overstimulation in social settings as a couple, ensuring that both partners feel comfortable and understood in social situations. Most importantly, we'll focus on how to respect the need for solitude without causing feelings of rejection, and how couples can tag-team social obligations with compassion and mutual support, especially during moments of social burnout.

The Introvert-Extrovert Spectrum Redefined by Neurodivergence

In traditional personality psychology, people are often categorized on a spectrum between introversion and extraversion. Introverts are typically seen as individuals who find energy in solitude and prefer more intimate, one-on-one interactions. Extraverts, on the other hand, are energized by socializing and thrive in larger group settings. However, when it comes to neurodivergence, this simple dichotomy doesn't always hold true.

For neurodivergent individuals, social needs are often more complex and nuanced. Autistic individuals, for instance, might experience social interactions with a level of intensity that can lead to overwhelming sensory and emotional input, while individuals with ADHD might have a fluctuating need for social stimulation—sometimes seeking connection to combat feelings of boredom, and other times becoming overstimulated by even the smallest social cues. Sensory processing disorders, common among neurodivergent individuals, can significantly impact a person's ability to engage in social activities. This means that while an extroverted neurotypical person might thrive in a bustling social setting, a neurodivergent individual could feel drained, overwhelmed, or even anxious in the same environment.

Instead of seeing the introvert-extrovert spectrum as a fixed trait, neurodivergence introduces the idea that social energy is fluid and varies depending on the individual's neurological makeup, sensory needs, and current emotional state. For example, an individual with ADHD may experience periods of heightened social energy, where they crave social interaction, but they may also go through phases of complete withdrawal when their attention is diverted by other tasks or stimuli. Similarly, an autistic person may enjoy socializing in small, controlled environments but may require longer periods of solitude to recharge afterward.

Redefining this spectrum in the context of neurodivergence means recognizing that social needs are highly individualized and can vary from one moment to the next. Understanding that the introvert-extrovert spectrum isn't a rigid classification but a shifting, fluid concept can help partners navigate the complexities of their relationship and better accommodate each other's social needs.

Managing Overstimulation in Social Settings as a Couple

Social overstimulation is a common challenge for many neurodivergent individuals, particularly those with autism or ADHD. Overstimulation occurs when sensory input—such as loud noises, bright lights, crowded spaces, or even the emotional intensity of a conversation—becomes too much to process, leading to feelings of anxiety, irritability, or emotional exhaustion. In social settings, this overstimulation can be overwhelming, especially when the neurodivergent individual's social battery is drained.

For couples, managing overstimulation in social situations involves creating a shared understanding of when and how to take breaks and how to respect each other's sensory boundaries.

- **Recognizing signs of overstimulation**: The first step is recognizing the physical and emotional signs of overstimulation. For instance, the neurodivergent partner may begin to exhibit signs of discomfort, such as fidgeting, withdrawing from conversation, or becoming unusually quiet or tense. The neurotypical partner should learn to recognize these signals and respond with empathy, offering the neurodivergent partner a chance to step away from the situation and take a break, even if it's just for a few minutes.

- **Pre-planning**: Before entering a social setting, couples can pre-plan strategies to minimize overstimulation. This might include agreeing on a signal or phrase that indicates the need to leave or take a break, ensuring that both partners feel comfortable in knowing when it's time to step away. For example, the neurodivergent partner might use a prearranged code word or gesture to indicate they're feeling overwhelmed. This ensures that the need for space is communicated respectfully and avoids any feelings of anxiety or frustration.

- **Creating safe spaces**: If attending social events is unavoidable, couples can create "safe spaces" where the neurodivergent partner can retreat to when needed. This might be a quiet room at a party, a designated spot in a restaurant, or even stepping outside for a few moments of fresh air. By establishing these spaces in advance, the couple can ensure that both partners feel comfortable and supported without causing disruptions or misunderstandings.

Navigating overstimulation as a couple requires patience, flexibility, and a willingness to adjust plans based on each partner's needs. In this way, couples can enjoy socializing while still respecting and accommodating each other's sensory boundaries.

Respecting the Need for Solitude Without Rejection

One of the most important aspects of maintaining a healthy neurodivergent relationship is respecting the need for solitude. Neurodivergent individuals, especially those on the autism spectrum or with ADHD, often require alone time to process emotions, manage sensory input, or simply recharge. While this is a normal part of neurodivergent life, it can sometimes be misinterpreted by the neurotypical partner as rejection or disconnection.

The need for solitude is not a reflection of a lack of love or affection. In fact, for many neurodivergent individuals, spending time alone is necessary for maintaining emotional well-being and for ensuring that they can continue to be emotionally present in their relationship. Without this alone time, they may become overstimulated, anxious, or burnt out, which can ultimately damage their ability to engage in the relationship meaningfully.

For neurotypical partners, it's important to understand that solitude is a form of self-care rather than a form of withdrawal. Rather than interpreting a partner's need for alone time as a personal rejection, the neurotypical partner should see it as a healthy and essential part of maintaining balance within the relationship. This understanding can help reduce feelings of insecurity or abandonment.

- **Communication is key**: To avoid misinterpretation, it's essential for both partners to communicate openly about the need for solitude. Instead of simply disappearing or retreating without explanation, the neurodivergent partner should express their need for space clearly. For instance, saying, "I need some quiet time to recharge so I can be fully present later," offers reassurance to the neurotypical partner that this isn't about the relationship but rather about personal needs.

- **Creating a supportive routine**: Couples can also create routines around solitude that accommodate both partners' needs. For example, setting aside specific times for personal downtime, such as reading, walking, or listening to music, ensures that both partners know they will have the space they need to recharge.

By respecting the need for solitude without taking it personally, both partners can strengthen their emotional connection and create a healthier, more balanced relationship.

Tag-Teaming Social Obligations with Compassion

Social obligations are a natural part of life, whether they are family gatherings, work events, or friend get-togethers. However, for neurodivergent individuals, social obligations can be a source of stress, anxiety, and exhaustion. In these situations, tag-teaming social events with compassion becomes an invaluable tool for managing social interactions as a couple.

Tag-teaming refers to the practice of working together as a team to manage social obligations, ensuring that both partners' needs are met while also fulfilling their social commitments. Here's how tag-teaming can be applied effectively:

- **Shared responsibility**: If attending a social event feels overwhelming for one partner, the other partner can step in to help navigate the event. For instance, the neurotypical partner can take the lead in greeting people, managing conversations, or handling logistics, allowing the neurodivergent partner to focus on their comfort level and emotional needs. This can alleviate the pressure of having to manage everything alone, making the experience more enjoyable for both.

- **Taking breaks together**: When social settings become overwhelming, tag-teaming can also involve taking breaks together. This might mean stepping outside for fresh air or finding a quiet corner to relax for a few moments. The key is to stay connected and supportive during these moments, ensuring that both partners feel cared for and understood.

- **Planning for downtime**: Tag-teaming social obligations also means planning for post-event downtime. After a social event, the neurodivergent partner may need a period of quiet time to decompress and recover. The neurotypical partner can support this by ensuring that the schedule allows for enough downtime and that there's no pressure to continue socializing if one partner is feeling burnt out.

By working together to manage social obligations with compassion and understanding, couples can navigate the challenges of socialization in a way that honors both partners' needs, ensuring that social events are fulfilling, not exhausting.

Conclusion

Navigating social needs and alone time in neurodivergent relationships requires a balance of understanding, compassion, and flexibility. By recognizing how neurodivergent traits—such as sensory sensitivity, time blindness, and fluctuating social energy—impact social engagement, couples can create a healthier, more supportive relationship dynamic. Respecting the need for solitude, managing overstimulation in social settings, and tag-teaming social obligations with empathy allows both partners to thrive without compromising their well-being.

In the end, love in a neurodivergent relationship is about respecting each other's rhythms—whether that means needing time alone to recharge or finding a way to engage in social activities without feeling overwhelmed. By approaching these needs with compassion, couples can build a relationship that is both fulfilling and sustainable, with room for both connection and personal space.

Chapter 9

Routines, Rituals, and Relationship Rhythms

How Structure Can Be the Love Language

For many neurodivergent individuals, routines and structure are not just helpful—they are essential. The predictability that routines provide can offer a sense of stability, reduce anxiety, and help manage sensory overload. Whether it's the comforting rhythm of daily rituals or the structured predictability of weekly activities, routine provides a framework that allows neurodivergent individuals to navigate their days with greater ease. However, in relationships, where two people's needs, personalities, and routines intersect, it's important to create systems that accommodate both partners' needs for structure and flexibility. In many ways, structure can become a love language, a way of expressing care, respect, and understanding.

In this chapter, we will explore how structure and routine can play a pivotal role in fostering intimacy and support in neurodivergent relationships. We will examine why certain neurodivergent individuals thrive on routines and how partners can help nurture and maintain them. We will discuss how creating daily, weekly, and emotional rituals can enhance the relationship, providing consistency and connection. Additionally, we'll explore how shared calendars and systems can reduce friction, especially in managing household responsibilities, social obligations, and time-sensitive tasks. Finally, we will delve into the challenge of negotiating the balance between flexibility and structure, acknowledging the varying needs of both neurotypical and neurodivergent partners.

Why Some Neurodivergent Folks Thrive on Routines— and How to Support That

For many neurodivergent individuals, especially those on the autism spectrum or with ADHD, the world can often feel unpredictable and overwhelming. Sensory overload, unexpected changes, or the challenge of managing time and tasks can lead to heightened stress, anxiety, or frustration. In these cases, routines provide a much-needed anchor. The predictability of daily schedules offers neurodivergent individuals a sense of control and safety, reducing uncertainty and making it easier to manage their daily tasks and emotions.

1. **Stability and predictability**: Routines offer a sense of stability that allows neurodivergent individuals to navigate their world with greater confidence. For example, someone with autism may prefer a set morning routine—waking up at the same time, following the same sequence of activities, and knowing what to expect. This predictable structure reduces anxiety and allows them to focus on other parts of their day without the added stress of uncertainty.

2. **Reducing decision fatigue**: Neurodivergent individuals often experience decision fatigue more intensely than neurotypical

individuals. Having routines in place can minimize the number of decisions that need to be made throughout the day, freeing up cognitive energy for more important tasks or emotional processing.

3. **Managing sensory overload**: Routines also help neurodivergent individuals manage sensory sensitivities. By creating environments that are familiar and controlled, such as a designated quiet space or a specific routine for winding down before bed, they can reduce the risk of sensory overload and make their environment more conducive to emotional regulation.

For neurotypical partners, supporting a neurodivergent loved one's need for routines can be an act of love. It's important to acknowledge and respect these routines rather than viewing them as inflexible or controlling. For example, if your partner needs a set time for breakfast or a structured approach to managing their workday, honoring these needs without judgment can go a long way in creating a supportive, understanding relationship.

Practical support might include:

- **Consistency**: Helping maintain the established routines, such as waking up at the same time, having a set morning ritual, or adhering to pre-agreed upon schedules for work or relaxation.

- **Clear communication**: Establishing routines that include regular check-ins or communication about upcoming changes, ensuring that the neurodivergent partner feels prepared for what's to come.

By embracing routines as a core part of the relationship, both partners can create a dynamic where predictability and stability are prioritized, ultimately leading to greater emotional security and connection.

Creating Daily, Weekly, and Emotional Rituals That Work for Both

Rituals are a powerful way to bond and create a sense of connection in relationships. In neurodivergent relationships, creating daily, weekly, and emotional rituals that accommodate both partners' needs for structure and flexibility can help deepen intimacy and reduce stress. These rituals are more than just routines—they are meaningful moments that reinforce connection and understanding.

1. **Daily Rituals**: Establishing daily rituals provides a sense of continuity and reassurance. This could be something as simple as sharing a morning coffee, exchanging a few moments of quiet time together before starting the day, or having a bedtime routine that involves unwinding together. For neurodivergent individuals, daily rituals can offer a predictable, safe environment where they feel emotionally supported and grounded.

   o **Example**: A couple could create a morning ritual where they spend five minutes chatting about the day ahead, providing clarity on schedules, or simply connecting emotionally before diving into the day's tasks. This kind of consistency can help both partners feel more attuned to each other, regardless of external stresses.

2. **Weekly Rituals**: Weekly rituals, such as a date night, a weekend chore day, or a family gathering, provide a recurring time for connection. For neurodivergent individuals, these rituals can help break the week into manageable segments, creating a sense of anticipation and security. These rituals also help partners maintain a sense of shared commitment and connection despite the busyness of everyday life.

   ○ **Example**: Setting aside one evening per week to focus solely on each other—whether it's a movie night, a dinner together, or a shared hobby—can offer both partners something to look forward to and reinforce their emotional bond. It's important to communicate in advance and ensure that this ritual feels comfortable for both individuals, with room for flexibility as needed.

3. **Emotional Rituals**: Emotional rituals help partners connect on a deeper level and create a sense of intimacy beyond physical interaction. These can include simple practices like checking in emotionally each day, expressing gratitude toward one another, or making time for heart-to-heart conversations. These rituals are particularly valuable in neurodivergent relationships, where communication may require extra effort and emotional regulation.

   ○ **Example**: An emotional ritual might involve asking each other, "How are you feeling today?" or using a specific phrase like "I appreciate you" or "Thank you for being patient with me." These small but powerful rituals can foster a deeper emotional understanding, promoting empathy and trust.

By creating and maintaining these rituals, couples can establish a rhythm that works for both individuals, ensuring that both partners feel heard, appreciated, and emotionally supported.

Making Shared Calendars and Systems That Reduce Friction

One of the most common sources of tension in relationships is the challenge of managing time and responsibilities. For neurodivergent individuals, particularly those with ADHD or executive dysfunction, keeping track of schedules, tasks, and commitments can be a significant source of stress. Shared calendars and systems help reduce friction in relationships by ensuring that both partners are on the same page and have a clear understanding of what needs to be done.

1. **Shared Calendars**: Using a shared digital calendar, such as Google Calendar or a couple's planner, can ensure that both partners are aware of important events, appointments, and commitments. This helps reduce the likelihood of missed events, last-minute scrambling, or forgotten responsibilities. For neurodivergent individuals with time blindness, a shared calendar offers visual reminders and helps create a structured framework for managing time.

- o **Example**: A couple might create a shared calendar where each partner adds work schedules, social events, family obligations, and personal appointments. This system allows both individuals to stay in sync and reduces the stress of having to manage everything independently.

2. **Task Management Systems**: In addition to a shared calendar, using a task management system—like a to-do list or project management tool—can help both partners stay organized and accountable. This could involve breaking down larger tasks into smaller, manageable steps, setting deadlines, and checking in with each other to ensure things are on track.

   - o **Example**: A couple could create a shared to-do list for household chores, where each partner is assigned specific tasks for the week. By using a digital tool or physical checklist, both partners can clearly see what needs to be done, minimizing misunderstandings and reducing the potential for task-related conflict.

3. **Routine Systems for Household Responsibilities**: Establishing clear systems for household duties, such as a rotating chore schedule, meal planning, or grocery shopping, can reduce the friction that arises when one partner feels like they are taking on more responsibility. For neurodivergent individuals, structure around these tasks provides clarity and helps reduce anxiety.

   - o **Example**: Setting up a weekly rotation of chores—such as one partner handling cleaning on Mondays and the other on Wednesdays—can help maintain fairness and ensure that tasks are not overlooked. Using visual reminders or checklists can also ensure that nothing is forgotten.

By using shared calendars and task management systems, couples can create a supportive framework for navigating daily life with less stress, ensuring that both partners feel equally involved in maintaining the relationship's balance.

Flexibility for One, Structure for the Other: Negotiating Needs

In many neurodivergent relationships, one partner may thrive on structure and routine, while the other may require more flexibility and spontaneity. Negotiating these different needs can be a challenge, but it's also an opportunity for growth and compromise.

1. **For the structured partner**: Neurodivergent individuals, especially those with ADHD or autism, may require more rigid routines and systems to help them manage their day. These individuals often rely on structure to reduce anxiety and stay organized. The neurotypical partner, in turn, may appreciate the security and predictability that structure provides in the relationship.

2. **For the flexible partner**: On the other hand, the neurotypical partner might have a more fluid approach to daily life, where spontaneity, flexibility, and open-ended plans are more

comfortable. They may resist rigid structures or need more room to improvise.

Negotiating these needs involves finding a middle ground where both partners feel respected and supported. It might involve compromise, such as setting aside time for spontaneous activities while also maintaining certain routines to ensure that both partners' needs are met.

- **Example**: One partner may agree to a structured daily routine for work or household responsibilities, while the other partner may propose that they leave weekends open for unplanned activities or relaxation. This balance allows for both routine and flexibility to coexist without sacrificing either partner's needs.

By recognizing and respecting the need for both flexibility and structure, couples can create a relationship rhythm that works for both partners—one that encourages growth, support, and mutual understanding.

Conclusion

Routines, rituals, and structure play a powerful role in neurodivergent relationships. For many neurodivergent individuals, structure provides stability, reduces anxiety, and creates a framework for success. For neurotypical partners, understanding and supporting these needs through shared calendars, task management systems, and daily rituals fosters a relationship that feels organized and emotionally supported.

By negotiating the balance between flexibility and structure, couples can navigate the complexities of neurodivergent life with compassion and understanding. When routine is embraced as a love language, it becomes more than just a tool for managing daily tasks—it becomes a meaningful expression of care, consideration, and commitment.

Chapter 10

Sensuality, Sex, and the Neurospicy Experience

Rewriting Intimacy for Sensory and Emotional Alignment

S ex and intimacy are central to many romantic relationships, serving as expressions of love, connection, and desire. However, when one or both partners are neurodivergent—whether with ADHD, autism, or other neurotypes—the experience of sensuality, sex, and intimacy can differ vastly from what is often portrayed in mainstream media or assumed in neurotypical relationships. For neurodivergent individuals, sensory sensitivities, emotional processing, and unique ways of experiencing connection can profoundly shape how they approach physical intimacy.

In this chapter, we will explore how to create a sensory-friendly and emotionally safe environment for intimacy in neurodivergent relationships. We'll discuss the importance of open communication about desire, boundaries, and arousal differences, and how these conversations can lead to a deeper understanding of each other's needs. We'll also look at how sex can be both a source of connection and, for some, a potential stressor—particularly when sensory overload or emotional dysregulation come into play. Finally, we'll bust common myths about neurodivergence and physical intimacy, showing that neurodivergent individuals can experience and express sexuality just as deeply and richly as anyone else.

Sensory-Friendly Sex and Emotional Safety

For many neurodivergent individuals, particularly those on the autism spectrum or with ADHD, sensory sensitivities can make physical intimacy a complex and sometimes overwhelming experience. Bright lights, strong smells, certain textures, or even the pressure of touch can lead to overstimulation, making intimacy feel uncomfortable, stressful, or even painful. For some, a lack of sensory control can make the idea of physical closeness anxiety-inducing, while for others, a heightened sensitivity may increase arousal and pleasure, but only within specific, controlled sensory environments.

Creating sensory-friendly sex involves adjusting the environment to ensure that both partners feel physically comfortable and emotionally safe. This might include:

1. **Control of lighting and sounds**: Dimmed lighting, soft music, or even the use of noise-canceling headphones can help reduce sensory overload during intimacy. Some neurodivergent individuals might prefer complete darkness or the absence of background noise, while others might enjoy certain types of ambient sounds that help them focus and relax.

2. **Tactile sensitivities**: Sensitivity to touch is a common experience in neurodivergent individuals. Textures of fabrics,

84

skin contact, and even the intensity of physical pressure can be overwhelming. For those with these sensitivities, choosing soft fabrics, experimenting with lighter or gentler touch, and gradually desensitizing the body to specific types of touch can be part of creating a safe space. Some may prefer to explore more gradual forms of touch, such as gentle caresses, soft massages, or even light brushing over the skin.

3. **Temperature control**: Heat or cold can significantly affect the comfort level during intimacy. Some neurodivergent individuals may be more sensitive to temperature changes, making it essential to adjust the room temperature, use blankets, or try temperature play (like warming up a cloth or using cool, smooth objects).

4. **Communication and boundaries**: For neurodivergent individuals, discussing sensory preferences and boundaries before engaging in intimacy is crucial. This conversation might be uncomfortable at first but is vital to ensuring that both partners feel safe and respected. Practicing non-judgmental communication about sensory needs—such as "I need softer touch" or "I prefer less pressure"—can significantly improve the experience of physical intimacy.

By creating a sensory-friendly environment, couples can allow space for more enjoyable and fulfilling intimacy, ensuring that both partners can engage in a way that respects their individual sensory needs.

Talking About Desire, Boundaries, and Arousal Differences

Sexuality is deeply personal, and neurodivergent individuals may have different experiences of desire, arousal, and intimacy than their neurotypical partners. Understanding these differences and openly communicating about sexual needs, desires, and boundaries is critical to fostering a healthy and respectful sexual relationship.

1. **Desire differences**: Neurodivergent individuals may experience desire differently from neurotypical individuals. For example, individuals with ADHD may have higher levels of impulsivity and may experience sexual desire that comes on suddenly and intensely but may struggle with maintaining consistent desire over time. On the other hand, individuals with autism might experience desire more sporadically, with intense periods of disinterest or emotional detachment in between moments of engagement. Understanding these patterns and acknowledging fluctuations in desire can help both partners feel more at ease without feeling that their sexual connection is in jeopardy.

2. **Arousal differences**: Arousal can also vary significantly between neurodivergent and neurotypical individuals. Sensory sensitivities can cause certain stimuli to be arousing or uncomfortable, while other neurodivergent individuals may require different kinds of stimulation—such as deep pressure, repetitive movements, or specific visual or auditory cues—to become aroused. Communicating these differences without shame is crucial.

3. **Setting clear boundaries**: For neurodivergent individuals, it's essential to establish clear boundaries about what is and isn't comfortable. This might include boundaries around touch, noise levels, or even the timing of intimate encounters. While these boundaries might shift depending on the partner's sensory state or emotional mood, honoring them creates a deeper sense of emotional safety and trust, reducing the likelihood of overstimulation or emotional burnout.

Practical tips for communication:

-   **Check-in conversations**: Before and after intimacy, having check-in conversations about what felt good, what didn't, and any adjustments that might be needed for next time is an essential part of maintaining intimacy. This allows both partners to understand each other's desires and adjust accordingly, making sex more enjoyable and emotionally fulfilling.

-   **Non-verbal communication**: For some neurodivergent individuals, speaking about intimate needs can feel uncomfortable or even overwhelming. In these cases, non-verbal communication—such as establishing visual signals or cues during intimacy—can be effective in expressing desires or discomfort without needing to interrupt the moment.

Sex as Connection vs. Stressor

In neurodivergent relationships, sex can be a source of connection, but it can also become a stressor, particularly when sensory overload, emotional dysregulation, or differing sexual needs are at play. The pressure to "perform" sexually can cause anxiety, and for some, sex may feel like a chore rather than a joyful, intimate expression of love. For others, physical intimacy might be used as a way to manage emotional needs, but it can inadvertently become a source of stress when emotional dysregulation or sensory sensitivities interfere.

1. **Sex as connection**: When approached thoughtfully and with an emphasis on mutual understanding and respect, sex can be a powerful tool for connection. It can help partners bond emotionally, foster physical closeness, and communicate love. For neurodivergent individuals, allowing space for non-traditional forms of intimacy—such as cuddling, mutual massages, or quiet companionship—can also contribute to deep emotional connection, even if sexual intercourse itself isn't the primary form of intimacy.

2. **Sex as a stressor**: If neurodivergent individuals feel overwhelmed by sensory input or anxious about potential misunderstandings in intimacy, sex can quickly become a source of stress. For instance, feeling pressured to "perform" sexually can exacerbate anxiety, especially if the neurodivergent individual is unable to meet their partner's expectations. Furthermore, if there is a lack of communication about sensory needs or arousal differences, the experience of intimacy can feel disjointed or even unpleasant.

Managing sex as a source of connection involves setting clear expectations, embracing different ways of connecting, and recognizing that intimacy is not always about physical sex. For neurodivergent couples, finding ways to enjoy intimacy without the stress of performing certain sexual acts is often key to creating a fulfilling relationship.

Busting Myths: Neurodivergence and Physical Intimacy

There are many myths surrounding neurodivergence and physical intimacy—particularly the assumption that neurodivergent individuals don't experience or desire sex in the same way as neurotypical individuals. These myths often perpetuate misunderstandings about sexual desire, arousal, and connection for neurodivergent individuals, leading to feelings of inadequacy, frustration, or shame.

1. **Myth #1: Neurodivergent individuals don't experience desire or arousal**: The idea that individuals with autism or ADHD do not experience sexual desire is a harmful misconception. Neurodivergent individuals can experience sexual desire, but the way they express or feel it may differ from neurotypical individuals. For example, someone with autism might experience sexual desire less frequently or in different circumstances but can still form deep, passionate emotional connections. Similarly, someone with ADHD might experience sudden, impulsive bursts of sexual desire, but may struggle with consistency over time.

2. **Myth #2: Neurodivergent individuals are uninterested in physical affection**: Another myth is that neurodivergent people,

particularly those with autism, are uninterested in physical affection. In reality, many neurodivergent individuals seek physical affection and intimacy in their own way. While they may have specific sensory needs or preferences, they still long for connection through touch, hugs, or sexual interaction. The key is respecting their sensory boundaries and finding ways to engage in physical closeness that feel comfortable for both partners.

3. **Myth #3: Neurodivergent sex is "unconventional" or "broken"**: There is a tendency to view neurodivergent sex as something that needs to be "fixed" or "corrected." The reality is that neurodivergent sex can be just as intimate, fulfilling, and passionate as any other. The way intimacy is experienced in neurodivergent relationships might look different, but it can be incredibly deep and meaningful when both partners communicate openly and respect each other's needs and boundaries.

By busting these myths, we can create a more inclusive understanding of neurodivergent sexuality—one that recognizes the diverse ways in which neurodivergent individuals experience and express sexual desire, pleasure, and intimacy.

Conclusion

Sensuality, sex, and intimacy in neurodivergent relationships are complex and deeply personal experiences. By creating sensory-friendly environments, engaging in open conversations about desire and boundaries, and challenging myths around neurodivergent sexuality, couples can create a relationship dynamic that is both fulfilling and supportive. Neurodivergent individuals experience love and connection through different lenses, and by embracing these differences, couples can cultivate a more intimate and enriching sexual relationship that honors each person's needs and desires. Rewriting intimacy isn't about conforming to traditional expectations—it's about creating a space where both partners feel comfortable, connected, and emotionally safe in their shared experience of love and sensuality.

Chapter 11

Masking and the Price of Pretending

When One (or Both) Partners Are Exhausted from Hiding

R omantic relationships thrive on authenticity, trust, and openness. Yet, for many neurodivergent individuals, the pressure to conform to societal norms and meet neurotypical expectations can create a barrier to authentic connection. The practice of masking—a coping mechanism where a neurodivergent individual hides or suppresses their true feelings, behaviors, and needs to fit in with the expectations of others—can be exhausting, isolating, and damaging, particularly when it extends into intimate relationships. For neurodivergent individuals, masking may seem like a necessary means of survival in a world that often doesn't understand or accommodate their needs. However, over time, the emotional toll of constantly pretending to be something one is not can take a severe toll on the individual's mental health, self-worth, and connection with their partner.

In this chapter, we will explore the profound impact of long-term masking in romantic relationships, particularly when one or both partners feel exhausted from constantly hiding their true selves. We will discuss how the act of masking affects intimacy, emotional connection, and personal identity. We'll explore the importance of creating an "unmasking safe zone," where both partners can show up authentically without fear of judgment or rejection. Finally, we'll address the emotional exhaustion, identity confusion, and the healing power of radical acceptance, and how couples can work together to create an environment where both individuals feel free to be their true selves.

The Impact of Long-Term Masking in Romantic Relationships

Masking is a survival strategy, a learned behavior that allows neurodivergent individuals to navigate a world that often expects conformity. It can manifest in many ways—imitating social behaviors, suppressing natural emotional responses, or attempting to hide traits associated with neurodivergence, such as repetitive movements, stimming, or difficulty with eye contact. While masking can provide short-term relief from social discomfort or discrimination, the long-term effects can be detrimental to mental and emotional well-being, particularly within the context of romantic relationships.

1. Emotional Exhaustion:

The act of constantly masking requires immense energy. For neurodivergent individuals, every interaction involves a mental calculation—deciding which parts of themselves to hide, what behaviors to suppress, and how to mimic neurotypical responses to social cues. Over time, this emotional labor accumulates, leading to exhaustion, burnout, and emotional depletion. In a romantic relationship, this exhaustion often goes unnoticed by the partner, as the neurodivergent individual may continue to function outwardly in a seemingly "normal" way. However, behind the mask, they may feel mentally and emotionally drained.

- **Example**: An autistic individual might suppress the urge to engage in stimming behaviors (like hand-flapping or repetitive movements) when in public or with their partner. While they may successfully suppress these behaviors in the moment, doing so over the long term creates a build-up of emotional fatigue. When they are home with their partner, they may feel the overwhelming need to retreat into solitude to recharge.

2. Identity Confusion:

One of the most insidious consequences of long-term masking is identity confusion. When neurodivergent individuals suppress their natural behaviors for long periods, they may begin to lose touch with their authentic selves. The constant pretending can lead to a disconnect between how they see themselves and how they believe they are perceived by others. In romantic relationships, this can result in a feeling of emotional disconnection, as the person feels that their partner is not truly getting to know the "real" them.

- **Example**: A neurodivergent partner may feel that their true identity is hidden beneath layers of "pretending." They may struggle with feelings of self-doubt, questioning if their partner loves them for who they truly are or for the version of themselves they have created to meet external expectations.

3. Suppressed Emotions and Unmet Needs:

When neurodivergent individuals mask their feelings, they often suppress their emotional needs as well. This can lead to frustration, resentment, and emotional withdrawal in the relationship. Unspoken needs—such as the need for downtime, alone time, or sensory accommodations—may go unnoticed by the partner, and as a result, they remain unmet. The partner doing the masking may feel emotionally isolated, even though they are physically present in the relationship.

- **Example**: An ADHD partner may mask their need for quiet or personal space during social events to avoid seeming rude or antisocial. Over time, the lack of recognition and accommodation for their needs can lead to emotional exhaustion and resentment toward their partner for not understanding their boundaries.

How to Create an "Unmasking Safe Zone"

For couples in neurodivergent relationships, creating an "unmasking safe zone" is an essential step in rebuilding emotional connection and fostering trust. This safe zone is a space where both partners can freely express their authentic selves without fear of judgment, rejection, or misunderstanding. It requires both individuals to actively work toward creating an emotionally supportive and understanding environment where vulnerability is embraced.

1. Open Communication and Radical Honesty:

The first step toward creating an unmasking safe zone is establishing open and honest communication. Both partners need to be able to express their needs, feelings, and desires in a way that is free from shame or fear of judgment. This can be challenging, especially for the neurodivergent partner, who may have spent a lifetime masking their emotions and desires. However, by fostering an environment where honesty is met with compassion and empathy, couples can begin to deconstruct the walls built by masking.

- **Example**: A neurodivergent partner might express, "I need some quiet time to recharge after a social event, or I may become overwhelmed. This isn't about not wanting to be with you; it's just that I need time to reset emotionally." This level of honesty allows the neurotypical partner to understand the need for solitude and provides space for understanding.

2. Radical Acceptance:

Radical acceptance involves embracing the neurodivergent partner's behaviors and needs without trying to change or fix them. It requires understanding that their way of experiencing the world is valid and that their emotional needs are just as important as those of the neurotypical partner. By accepting each other's quirks, sensory preferences, and emotional responses, both partners can create a safer space where masking is no longer necessary.

- **Example**: If one partner has a sensory sensitivity that makes certain textures, smells, or sounds unbearable, radical acceptance means respecting those sensitivities without judgment. This may involve making adjustments in the living space or discussing ways to navigate social events that respect these needs.

3. Creating Rituals for Unmasking:

Building rituals around unmasking can help normalize the process of letting go of societal expectations and fully embracing authenticity. This can include creating regular moments where both partners are encouraged to share their feelings, concerns, and vulnerabilities openly. These rituals foster emotional safety, making it easier for both partners to express themselves without fear of rejection.

- **Example**: A couple might establish a nightly ritual where, before going to bed, they share one thing that went well that day and one thing that felt challenging. This simple act of sharing builds emotional intimacy and allows both partners to be vulnerable with each other, knowing that their feelings will be accepted without judgment.

Emotional Exhaustion, Identity Confusion, and Radical Acceptance

The emotional toll of masking can create a sense of exhaustion and identity confusion, as neurodivergent individuals may feel lost in the process of constantly pretending. The pressure to hide one's true self can lead to burnout, low self-esteem, and a sense of disconnection in the relationship.

1. Emotional Exhaustion:

As discussed earlier, the emotional labor of masking can lead to burnout. This exhaustion manifests not only physically but also emotionally, as the individual may feel emotionally drained by the effort of constantly maintaining a facade. Emotional exhaustion in a relationship can result in detachment, irritability, and an overall lack of energy for intimacy and connection.

- **Example**: A partner might feel emotionally distant from their neurodivergent loved one, sensing that something is "off" but unsure why. The neurodivergent individual may struggle to communicate the fatigue they feel from constantly pretending to fit in, leading to feelings of isolation in the relationship.

2. Identity Confusion:

The constant act of masking can lead to identity confusion for the neurodivergent individual. Over time, they may begin to question who they truly are when their authentic self is hidden beneath layers of adaptation and conformity. This disconnection from their true identity can create deep inner conflict and self-doubt.

- **Example**: A neurodivergent partner may feel uncertain about their own preferences, desires, and needs because they have spent so much time suppressing them to please others. They may feel lost, wondering who they are when they are no longer masking for the benefit of others.

3. Radical Acceptance in Relationships:

Radical acceptance of each other's differences is the key to overcoming emotional exhaustion and identity confusion. This involves embracing the neurodivergent partner's true self, acknowledging the difficulties they face in a world that isn't designed for them, and supporting them in their journey toward self-discovery and authenticity.

- ■ **Example**: A neurotypical partner may come to understand that their neurodivergent loved one struggles with certain social interactions but doesn't blame them for it. Instead, they offer reassurance and support, recognizing that the neurodivergent partner is doing their best within the constraints of their unique brain wiring.

Radical acceptance requires patience, understanding, and a deep sense of empathy. It means embracing each other for who you truly are, imperfections and all, and learning to love each other with all the rawness, authenticity, and vulnerability that comes with shedding the mask.

Relearning How to Show Up Authentically

Relearning how to show up authentically in a relationship is a process that requires time, patience, and practice. For neurodivergent individuals who have spent years or even decades masking their true selves, this process can feel overwhelming. It involves unlearning patterns of behavior that were once necessary for survival and embracing a new way of relating to oneself and one's partner.

1. Taking Small Steps:

The process of unmasking doesn't happen overnight. It involves taking small steps toward self-acceptance and vulnerability. Each time the neurodivergent individual allows themselves to be authentically seen, they move closer to reclaiming their true identity. For the neurotypical partner, this means being patient and supportive as their loved one navigates this journey.

- **Example**: The neurodivergent partner might start by sharing small vulnerabilities, such as expressing a need for alone time or asking for help with managing sensory overload. Over time, these small acts of authenticity can build trust and strengthen the emotional bond between partners.

2. Building a New Relationship Dynamic:

As both partners engage in the process of unmasking, the relationship dynamic itself may shift. The couple will begin to create new patterns of interaction based on authenticity and mutual respect rather than pretending or conforming to external expectations. This shift can feel liberating, as both individuals embrace the freedom to express their true selves without fear of judgment.

- **Example**: As both partners show up authentically, they may find that their emotional connection deepens, and their intimacy becomes more genuine. The neurodivergent partner no longer feels the need to hide their true feelings, while the neurotypical partner learns to embrace and appreciate their loved one's unique needs and behaviors.

Conclusion

Long-term masking can take a significant emotional toll on neurodivergent individuals in relationships. It leads to exhaustion, identity confusion, and emotional burnout. However, through the practice of radical acceptance, open communication, and the creation of an "unmasking safe zone," couples can begin to unravel the layers of pretending and cultivate a deeper, more authentic connection. By relearning how to show up authentically, both partners can foster a relationship that honors individuality, vulnerability, and mutual respect.

Society often pressures neurodivergent individuals to conform, the ability to unmask within a safe, supportive relationship is a profound act of love. It is a process of shedding societal expectations and embracing the beauty of authenticity, where both partners can fully be themselves without fear of rejection. Through this journey, couples can build a relationship based on genuine connection, emotional safety, and mutual growth.

Chapter 12

Crisis Mode—Handling Shutdowns, Meltdowns, and Relationship Overwhelm

How to Love During the Hardest Moments

Every relationship faces its share of challenges, but when one or both partners are neurodivergent, those challenges can sometimes feel insurmountable, especially during moments of emotional dysregulation. Neurodivergent individuals, particularly those with conditions like autism, ADHD, and sensory processing disorders, may experience shutdowns or meltdowns—intense emotional responses to sensory overload, stress, or emotional overwhelm. These moments can be difficult for both the neurodivergent individual and their partner to navigate, often leading to feelings of frustration, confusion, and even alienation.

However, these moments don't have to spell the end of connection. In fact, how a couple responds to these emotional crises can shape the strength of their relationship, providing opportunities for deeper empathy, mutual support, and healing. Understanding the early signs of overwhelm, knowing how to respond during emotional overload, and having effective repair strategies in place can help both partners weather these emotional storms with compassion and grace.

In this chapter, we will explore the nature of shutdowns, meltdowns, and relationship overwhelm, offering practical tools for identifying early signs of emotional dysregulation and providing guidance on how to manage these moments in a way that strengthens the relationship. We will also discuss effective repair strategies for rebuilding trust and emotional safety after a crisis and provide insights into creating a couple's crisis toolkit that equips both partners to handle challenging moments together.

Identifying Early Signs of Overwhelm

Recognizing the early signs of overwhelm is crucial for both partners in a neurodivergent relationship. Overwhelm can manifest in various ways—emotionally, physically, or behaviorally—and identifying these signs early on can help prevent escalation into a meltdown or shutdown. For neurodivergent individuals, being aware of their own signs of distress is key, but it's equally important for their partner to recognize when something is starting to go wrong.

1. Subtle Physical and Behavioral Changes:

Before an emotional overload occurs, the neurodivergent partner may exhibit physical or behavioral signs that indicate they are starting to feel overwhelmed. These signs can be subtle but are crucial for early intervention. Some common early warning signs include:

- **Restlessness or agitation**: The neurodivergent partner might start fidgeting, pacing, or exhibiting repetitive movements.

- **Change in facial expressions**: There may be a visible shift in mood, such as furrowed brows, clenched fists, or a tense jaw.

- **Difficulty making eye contact**: The neurodivergent partner might start avoiding eye contact, signaling emotional withdrawal.

- **Increased sensitivity to sensory stimuli**: Loud sounds, bright lights, or even certain smells may become increasingly intolerable.

2. Verbal Signs of Discomfort:

In some cases, the neurodivergent partner may express discomfort verbally before reaching a crisis point. These early verbal cues might include:

- **Short or clipped responses**: The neurodivergent individual may start giving one-word answers or seem distracted in conversations.

- **Irritability or frustration**: Small things may start to irritate them, leading to verbal expressions of frustration or annoyance.

- **Requests for space**: If they begin to say things like "I need a break" or "Can we just stop for a moment?" it's a sign they're reaching the limit of their emotional capacity.

3. Increased Sensory Sensitivity:

For many neurodivergent individuals, sensory overload is one of the leading causes of emotional dysregulation. If the neurodivergent partner starts showing signs of sensory discomfort—such as holding their ears, covering their eyes, or seeking quiet places—it's an indication that they are beginning to feel overwhelmed.

As a partner, it's essential to pay attention to these subtle signs. Being proactive in addressing early overwhelm can help prevent escalation into a full-blown meltdown or shutdown. Once these early signs are recognized, the neurotypical partner can step in with gentle support and encouragement, helping the neurodivergent partner manage their sensory input or emotional state before it becomes too overwhelming.

What to Do (and What Not to Do) During Emotional Overloads

When one partner enters crisis mode—whether it's a shutdown, meltdown, or intense emotional overwhelm—it can be a highly charged, unpredictable moment. Both partners need to understand how to manage the situation with care, patience, and empathy. Knowing what to do and what not to do during emotional overload can make the difference between a moment of conflict and a moment of connection.

1. What to Do:

- **Stay Calm and Grounded**: The most important thing during an emotional overload is to remain calm and grounded. Emotional regulation is contagious—if the neurotypical partner remains calm and supportive, it can help the neurodivergent partner regain composure more quickly. Take deep breaths, maintain a soft tone, and avoid escalating the situation with your own frustration or anxiety.

- **Offer Physical Space**: For some neurodivergent individuals, having space is crucial when they're overwhelmed. If the partner shows signs of withdrawing, give them physical space to process their emotions. For others, a reassuring touch like a hand on their back or holding their hand can provide comfort. Respect their preference—some may need space, while others may seek physical closeness.

- **Offer Reassurance**: In the heat of a meltdown or shutdown, it's important to offer reassurance. Acknowledge their experience with compassionate statements like, "I'm here with you," or "Take your time, we'll figure this out together." Let them know that their emotional experience is valid and that they're not alone in facing it.

- **Use Calming Strategies**: Depending on the needs of the neurodivergent partner, you can introduce calming strategies to help regulate their emotions. This could include dimming the lights, lowering noise levels, or guiding them through deep breathing exercises. Sensory tools, like soft textures, fidget toys, or noise-canceling headphones, can be useful in moments of sensory overwhelm.

- **Empathize and Validate**: Listen to their emotions without judgment. Instead of trying to fix the problem, validate their feelings. For example, saying "I can see you're feeling overwhelmed, and that's okay. Let's figure out what you need" can go a long way in helping them feel understood.

2. What Not to Do:

- **Don't Argue or Debate**: In the middle of a meltdown or shutdown, it's important not to engage in a debate or argument. Trying to rationalize or reason with the person during an emotional overload can exacerbate the situation. Avoid statements like, "Why are you acting like this?" or "You're overreacting." These comments are dismissive and can increase emotional distress.

- **Don't Force Communication**: If the neurodivergent partner is in a shutdown or emotionally overwhelmed, forcing them to communicate when they're not ready will likely increase their stress. Allow them time and space to recover, and only engage in conversation when they feel ready.

- **Don't Take It Personally**: Emotional overloads, especially meltdowns, can lead to verbal or physical expressions of frustration. Remember that this is not a personal attack. In these moments, it's crucial to remind yourself that their reaction is likely due to sensory overload, emotional dysregulation, or other neurodivergent factors, not because of something you've done wrong.

- **Don't Offer Unsolicited Solutions**: While it's natural to want to help, offering unwanted solutions during a meltdown or shutdown can feel overwhelming and intrusive. Instead, ask if they need help or if there's something you can do to support them. Offering open-ended support ("How can I help?") is more effective than jumping in with suggestions.

Repair Strategies and Rebuilding Trust After Dysregulated Moments

Even after emotional crises pass, the work of rebuilding trust and emotional connection is essential. If the neurodivergent partner's emotional dysregulation led to hurtful words or actions, or if the neurotypical partner felt dismissed or neglected, both partners need to engage in repair strategies to restore trust and intimacy.

1. Acknowledge the Impact of the Crisis:

After the emotional overload has passed, it's important to acknowledge the impact the crisis may have had on both individuals. A simple statement like, "I know that was really hard for both of us," or "I'm sorry that I couldn't support you in the way you needed," helps open the door to emotional repair. The key is not to place blame, but to acknowledge the experience with empathy.

2. Offer a Genuine Apology:

If the neurodivergent partner has said something hurtful during a meltdown or shutdown, offering a genuine apology is crucial. This isn't about apologizing for their neurodivergence, but rather for any behavior that might have caused distress. Similarly, if the neurotypical partner feels hurt, they can also express their feelings and apologize if needed.

3. Reaffirm Your Commitment:

During moments of crisis, it's easy for both partners to feel disconnected or isolated. Reaffirming your commitment to the relationship can help restore emotional safety. For example, saying, "I'm here for you, no matter what," or "We'll get through this together," helps both partners feel supported and valued.

4. Engage in Repair Rituals:

Couples may also create rituals for emotional repair that help them reconnect after a crisis. This might involve taking a walk together, sitting down for a quiet conversation, or simply holding hands in a moment of calm. These rituals can help restore intimacy and provide a sense of emotional security.

Developing Your Couple's "Crisis Toolkit"

Building a crisis toolkit—a set of tools and strategies that both partners can use when emotional crises arise—can help prevent misunderstandings and emotional burnout. A crisis toolkit should be personalized to the needs of both partners, incorporating strategies that have worked well in the past.

1. Pre-emptive Strategies:

Having a shared understanding of triggers—both personal and relational—can help prevent emotional overload from escalating. Discuss potential stressors, such as social events, work pressure, or sensory sensitivities, and agree on how to navigate them together.

2. Emotional Regulation Techniques:

Both partners should be familiar with techniques for managing stress and emotional dysregulation. This might include grounding exercises, mindfulness practices, or the use of sensory tools like calming music or weighted blankets.

3. Emergency Communication Signals:

Developing a non-verbal signal or phrase to indicate when one partner needs space or is beginning to feel overwhelmed can help diffuse potential crises early. This communication strategy ensures that both partners understand each other's needs without added emotional pressure.

4. Post-Crisis Check-ins:

After each emotional crisis, setting aside time to check in with each other about what worked, what didn't, and what could be improved is essential. This ongoing dialogue strengthens the relationship and ensures that both partners feel heard, supported, and valued.

Conclusion

Crisis moments—whether they involve shutdowns, meltdowns, or emotional overwhelm—are an inevitable part of many neurodivergent relationships. However, these challenges don't have to drive a wedge between partners. By identifying early signs of overwhelm, responding with empathy and support, and employing effective repair strategies, couples can navigate emotional crises with greater understanding and resilience.

Creating a crisis toolkit tailored to the needs of both partners ensures that they have the tools to weather difficult moments and rebuild trust after emotional dysregulation. With patience, empathy, and a shared commitment to emotional safety, couples can transform these moments of crisis into opportunities for growth, deeper connection, and mutual support.

Through compassionate communication, active emotional regulation, and a willingness to face challenges together, couples can foster a relationship that is not only strong in times of crisis but also deeply rooted in understanding, acceptance, and love.

Chapter 13

Wired for Growth—Strong, Loving, and Neurodivergent Together

The Future You Can Build on Your Own Terms

Society often feels like it's designed for the majority; neurodivergent individuals and their partners sometimes find themselves navigating a path that's uniquely their own. While traditional relationships have often been defined by societal norms and standardized expectations, neurodivergent couples have the opportunity to redefine what love, growth, and partnership look like—on their own terms. The truth is, neurodivergence doesn't have to be an obstacle to love, connection, or success. In fact, when embraced with the right mindset and tools, neurodivergent relationships can thrive in ways that many never imagined.

In this chapter, we're going to explore the ways that neurodivergent couples are building strong, loving, and resilient relationships, not despite their differences, but because of them. By acknowledging and understanding the unique dynamics that neurodivergence brings into a relationship, couples can grow together in ways that are rich with opportunity and growth. We will dive into success stories, explore how to maintain humor, joy, and wonder in your relationship, and examine how mental health maintenance and couples therapy can work for neurodivergent couples. Lastly, we'll look at how embracing differences rather than shying away from them can lead to deeper understanding, stronger connections, and a partnership that is truly built on mutual growth.

By the end of this chapter, you'll have a better understanding of how to navigate your neurodivergent relationship in a way that promotes growth, strengthens your bond, and allows you to thrive together—on your terms.

Success Stories: Neurodivergent Couples Thriving Together

One of the most inspiring aspects of neurodivergent relationships is the sheer variety of ways that couples can thrive. Whether you are on the autism spectrum, have ADHD, dyslexia, or any other form of neurodivergence, there are countless success stories of couples who have embraced their differences, adapted to each other's needs, and created partnerships that are thriving. These stories are proof that neurodivergent relationships are not only possible—they can be incredibly fulfilling.

1. **The Power of Understanding**: Take the example of Sarah and David, both of whom are neurodivergent. Sarah, who is on the autism spectrum, struggled with the nuances of social communication, especially in relationships. David, who has ADHD, often found himself overwhelmed by distractions and scattered thoughts. In the beginning, their differences created tension in their relationship. However, through open communication and a deep understanding of each other's needs,

they were able to find strategies that worked for them. For Sarah, this meant setting clear expectations and routines, which helped her feel secure. For David, it meant finding ways to organize his thoughts and reduce distractions during key moments of their relationship.

2. Their story is an example of how, with patience and understanding, two neurodivergent individuals can thrive together. The key was recognizing that their challenges didn't define them; instead, they used their differences as a platform to create a partnership that was built on mutual support and growth.

3. **Embracing Neurodivergence as a Strength**: Another couple, Mark and Lisa, show how embracing neurodivergence can strengthen a relationship. Mark has ADHD, and Lisa has dyslexia. Early on, Mark would often interrupt Lisa during conversations, thinking of multiple things at once, while Lisa would become frustrated with his disorganized approach to tasks. Initially, these differences led to misunderstandings. But instead of seeing these traits as problems, Mark and Lisa decided to embrace their neurodivergence as strengths. They developed a system where Mark would use visual reminders and timers to stay on track, and Lisa would write down her thoughts in lists, making her ideas more clear. They learned to work together by leaning into their neurodivergence, each finding ways to complement the other's thinking.

4. Their success wasn't about fixing their differences, but about understanding and adapting to them. By creating a supportive, collaborative space for each other, they grew stronger as a couple, making their neurodivergent traits an integral part of their love story rather than something to be ashamed of.

Keeping Humor, Joy, and Wonder Alive in Your Unique Love Story

Neurodivergent relationships are often characterized by humor, creativity, and an unexpected sense of joy. While neurodivergence may come with challenges, it also brings a unique flavor to love and connection. The key is finding the humor and wonder in your differences rather than allowing them to be a source of frustration or isolation.

1. **Laugh at the Little Things**: One of the best ways neurodivergent couples can stay grounded and maintain their connection is by finding humor in their unique perspectives. Neurodivergent partners often have different ways of seeing the world, and these differences can lead to moments of unexpected humor. Whether it's the way you organize your home, the quirky habits you've developed, or your unique way of communicating, taking the time to laugh together can diffuse tension and strengthen your bond.

   o **Example**: Take the example of Ella and Jack. Ella has ADHD, and Jack has autism. Their communication styles are very different—Ella tends to speak quickly, jump from topic to topic, and can get easily distracted, while

Jack prefers slow, deliberate conversations and dislikes interruptions. At first, this led to misunderstandings and frustration. However, over time, Ella and Jack learned to laugh at their communication quirks. When Ella would jump from topic to topic, Jack would humorously say, "Are we on a scavenger hunt? What's the next clue?" This playfulness helped them embrace their differences and maintain a sense of joy and spontaneity in their relationship.

2. **Create Rituals of Connection**: Neurodivergent couples often benefit from creating rituals that support connection and emotional intimacy. These rituals could be anything from having regular check-ins to spending quality time together through shared activities. The key is to make sure that your rituals are tailored to your unique needs as a couple, allowing for moments of joy, relaxation, and mutual understanding.

   o **Example**: Emily and Michael, a neurodivergent couple, established a "tech-free" night every week, where they would turn off their phones, play board games, and have uninterrupted conversations. This simple ritual allowed them to connect emotionally without the distractions of the outside world, strengthening their relationship and deepening their bond.

Mental Health Maintenance and Couples Therapy That Works

Mental health is a critical part of any relationship, but for neurodivergent couples, it can sometimes feel like an extra layer of complexity. Navigating mental health issues within the context of neurodivergence requires understanding, flexibility, and the right tools for emotional support.

1. **Mental Health Maintenance**: Just as you would maintain physical health with exercise and nutrition, maintaining mental health is essential for long-term relationship success. This includes practicing self-care, emotional regulation, and mental wellness practices.

   ○ **Self-Care for Neurodivergent Partners**: Each person's self-care routine should align with their neurodivergent needs. For example, if one partner has ADHD, setting up routines and using tools like timers or planners can reduce overwhelm. If one partner has anxiety or autism, taking time for deep relaxation, mindfulness, or creating a quiet space for decompression may be essential. Neurodivergent couples should work together to support each other's mental health and create a balanced environment that nurtures well-being.

2. **Therapy That Works for Neurodivergent Couples**: Traditional couples therapy may not always cater to the unique needs of neurodivergent couples, but that doesn't mean therapy

isn't a viable option. It's crucial to find a therapist who understands neurodivergence and can tailor sessions to your specific needs as a couple.

- ○ **Therapist-Client Fit**: Neurodivergent couples should seek therapists who are not only understanding of the challenges that neurodivergence can bring to a relationship but who also respect the individual needs of each partner. Whether it's having structured sessions, using visual aids, or providing clear and direct communication strategies, a tailored approach can ensure that therapy is beneficial.

- ○ **Couples Therapy Techniques**: Cognitive Behavioral Therapy (CBT), Schema Therapy, and couples counseling focused on communication strategies are effective for neurodivergent couples. These therapies can help couples understand each other's cognitive and emotional needs, develop better communication strategies, and address specific relationship challenges.

Growing Not in Spite of Your Differences—but Because of Them

The most powerful shift neurodivergent couples can make is changing the narrative from "we are different, and we have to deal with it" to "we are different, and that makes us stronger." The strengths that come from neurodivergence—creativity, attention to detail, unique problem-solving skills—can be a valuable asset in a relationship, as long as both partners are open to growth, understanding, and mutual support.

1. **Harnessing Strengths**: Neurodivergent individuals often have unique strengths that, when harnessed in a relationship, can bring about incredible growth. For example, a partner with autism may have exceptional attention to detail, which can help the couple stay organized, plan better, and manage projects more effectively. A partner with ADHD may bring an element of spontaneity and creativity to the relationship, keeping things fresh and exciting. Instead of seeing these differences as hindrances, neurodivergent couples can embrace them as strengths that can push their relationship to new heights.

2. **Celebrating Differences**: The key to growing as a couple lies in embracing, rather than fighting, your differences. When you acknowledge each other's unique perspectives and qualities, you begin to build a foundation of respect and trust. This doesn't mean ignoring challenges, but rather facing them together as a team. The goal is not to change each other, but to grow together by building on the strengths that each partner brings to the table.

Conclusion:

Neurodivergent couples have the power to create relationships that are uniquely their own—relationships that are rich with depth, understanding, and growth. By embracing their differences, maintaining humor, investing in mental health, and finding the right support systems, neurodivergent couples can build a future that is based on mutual respect and love, on their own terms.

As you journey forward, remember that the true beauty of any partnership lies in the ability to adapt, grow, and thrive together. Neurodivergence may introduce challenges, but it also provides an opportunity for transformation, connection, and the creation of a truly unique love story. Whether you're just beginning your journey or are already well along the way, know that you are capable of building a relationship that is stronger, richer, and more fulfilling because of your differences.

Epilogue

Navigating the intricacies of a neurodivergent relationship can feel like a lifelong journey—one full of challenges, but also rich in growth, learning, and deep connection. Throughout this book, we have explored the unique experiences of neurodivergent couples, examining both the struggles and the joys of building a lasting partnership when one or both partners are neurodivergent. We have covered the complexities of neurodivergence—from the impact of ADHD and autism to sensory sensitivities, emotional regulation, and everything in between. Along the way, we've discussed how these differences can sometimes create tension but, more importantly, how they can be embraced to build something truly beautiful, resilient, and full of love.

From the very beginning, it became clear that neurodivergent relationships do not need to conform to societal norms or follow the traditional scripts of romantic partnerships. Instead, they offer the potential to forge new paths that work for both partners—paths shaped by understanding, mutual respect, and a willingness to grow and adapt together. Neurodivergence does not equal dysfunction or limitation; it is simply a different way of experiencing the world. And when embraced fully, it offers an opportunity for a relationship that is as unique and profound as the individuals who create it.

Throughout our discussions, we've recognized the importance of creating a safe space for both partners to express their true selves. Masking, a behavior common among neurodivergent individuals, can be exhausting and lead to emotional burnout, identity confusion, and relational strain. But when partners work together to build an environment where both feel comfortable "unmasking," they can break free from the weight of pretending, leading to more authentic and meaningful connections. By acknowledging each other's differences and developing strategies to handle emotional overload, sensory sensitivities, and moments of crisis, neurodivergent couples can move beyond mere survival into thriving together.

The chapters on emotional dysregulation, shutdowns, and meltdowns highlighted the intense emotional landscapes that neurodivergent individuals often navigate. While these moments can be challenging, they don't define the relationship. Instead, they offer an opportunity for the couple to come together and practice empathy, patience, and understanding. Learning how to recognize the early signs of overwhelm and knowing what to do (and what not to do) during these emotional crises can make all the difference. Repair strategies—honoring each other's emotional needs and rebuilding trust after difficult moments—are vital for keeping the relationship strong. Crisis management isn't about avoiding conflict but about learning to handle it with love and care.

At the heart of every neurodivergent relationship is the desire to connect and create something lasting. Whether through daily rituals, shared hobbies, or spontaneous adventures, couples can keep humor, joy, and wonder alive in their love story. Recognizing that laughter can defuse tension and that shared moments of beauty can create lasting memories helps neurodivergent couples stay connected even in the face of challenges. This connection is built on the foundation of radical acceptance, where both partners honor their individual neurodivergence without judgment and love each other for who they truly are.

We've also addressed the importance of mental health and therapy. While neurodivergent couples can navigate their unique challenges on their own, seeking professional help—whether through couples therapy or individual support—can provide invaluable tools for communication, conflict resolution, and emotional regulation. Building a healthy, sustainable relationship requires continuous effort and self-care, but with the right tools, both partners can thrive individually and together.

Ultimately, the journey of growth in neurodivergent relationships isn't about overcoming differences—it's about embracing them. By learning to communicate effectively, respecting each other's sensory needs, and honoring boundaries, neurodivergent couples create a relationship that works for them. Their differences are not obstacles to intimacy; they are the building blocks of a connection that is strong, loving, and deeply fulfilling.

As you reflect on the chapters of this book, remember that neurodivergent relationships are not defined by the challenges they face but by the love and strength that emerge from navigating those challenges together. With empathy, patience, and a commitment to authenticity, couples can create a future full of shared experiences, emotional connection, and personal growth. The future you build together is not one you have to fit into a conventional mold—it is one that is uniquely yours, a love story written on your own terms, full of beauty, depth, and the power to thrive.

www.ingramcontent.com/pod-product-compliance
Lightning Source LLC
Chambersburg PA
CBHW071517120626

46550CB00006B/2255